A NATURAL HISTORY OF LAKE COUNTY, OHIO

Edited by

Rosemary N. Szubski

Published by:	The Cleveland Museum of Natural History © 1993 Cleveland, Ohio 44106
Produced by:	The Cleveland Museum of Natural History, Lake Metroparks, and The Holden Arboretum
Project Managers:	Rosemary Szubski and Stephen Madewell
Graphic Design, Photo Scans and Corrections, Info-Graphics and Production:	Vance J. Wissinger, Jr. Westendorf Printing
Printing:	Westendorf Printing
Cover Photos:	Ian Adams Photography — Headlands Beach — Paine Falls — Shipman Pond — Big Creek

ISBN   1-878600-06-0

Foreword

Although Lake County is the smallest county in Ohio, it has a broad spectrum of remarkably diverse natural features. Bound on the north by the Lake Erie shoreline, Lake County boasts within its boundaries sandy beaches and dunes, delicate wetlands, two major scenic rivers, steep ravines, broad valleys, sweeping meadows, deep hardwood forests and spectacular rock cliffs. Equally diverse are the plant communities and wildlife that inhabit each area.

The natural history of Lake County is a complex story that includes both the dynamics of natural phenomena and the effects of human activity. Lake County's abundant natural resources and geographic location make it a prime area for settlement. Over the past 200 years, increasing numbers of people have been using its resources, changing its landscape and altering its environment.

To heighten community awareness and appreciation for the county's natural assets, the 1940 Lake County Centennial Committee published a 32 page booklet, *A Natural History of Lake County, Ohio*, "to call attention to the beauties and natural features of which we are exorbitantly proud." The booklet noted Lake County geology and natural resources, listed plants, birds and mammals, and promoted the concept of setting aside pristine areas in the county as wildlife sanctuaries.

In the foreword to the 1940 Centennial booklet, C. M. Shipman stated, "Living things may be symbols of the past worthy of our love and admiration along with those inanimate man-made objects which we treasure in our museums. I feel this is the prime reason for *A Natural History of Lake County, Ohio*." That message is still true today. The more we learn about natural history, the more we come to understand that conserved natural areas are living museums that continually teach us about our relationship to the natural environment.

A totally comprehensive review of the natural history of Lake County could fill volumes. This publication expands the scope of that earlier booklet and is intended to be an updated, introductory overview that includes recent changes in land use which have made a marked impact on the landscape of Lake County. It is hoped that readers of this guidebook will be surprised, awed, amused and inspired.

Dramatic changes have occurred in Lake County since the 1940 Centennial celebration. Now, more than ever, it is important to respect and conserve fragile environments and resources in Lake County so that future generations will also come to know and enjoy its remarkable natural assets.

A Natural History

of Lake County, Ohio

Table of Contents

Getting Acquainted with Lake County

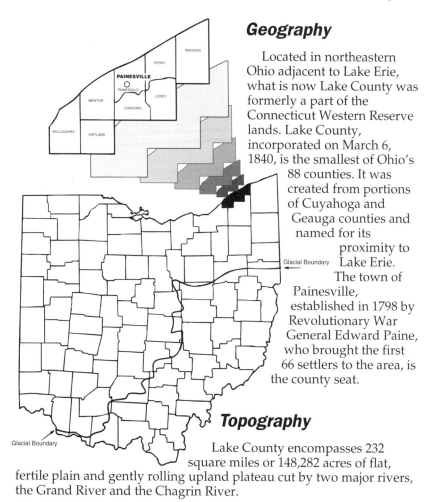

Geography

Located in northeastern Ohio adjacent to Lake Erie, what is now Lake County was formerly a part of the Connecticut Western Reserve lands. Lake County, incorporated on March 6, 1840, is the smallest of Ohio's 88 counties. It was created from portions of Cuyahoga and Geauga counties and named for its proximity to Lake Erie.

The town of Painesville, established in 1798 by Revolutionary War General Edward Paine, who brought the first 66 settlers to the area, is the county seat.

Topography

Lake County encompasses 232 square miles or 148,282 acres of flat, fertile plain and gently rolling upland plateau cut by two major rivers, the Grand River and the Chagrin River.

These natural topographical contrasts, enhanced by erosion and glacial action, contribute to Lake County's beauty, climate, resources and varied natural environments.

Lake County is situated in two distinct physiographic regions. A three-to-five mile wide flat region to the north, paralleling the Lake Erie shoreline, is known as the lake plain. The south/southeastern highland regions of the county (Willoughby Hills, Waite Hill, Concord, Leroy, southern Perry Township and southern Madison Township) are on the Allegheny Plateau. The transition area between the two regions is the rising Portage Escarpment which crosses the county in a roughly northeast/southwest line.

6

The Lake Plain

Along the northern edge of the lake plain are the Lake Erie shoreline bluffs, which rise 30 to 70 feet above the lake. The bluffs offer a magnificent view of the lake, but form a nearly continuous cliff that inhibits access to the lake except where major rivers and streams have cut through. Bluff areas along the shoreline can range from an irregular steep slope to a vertical cliff.

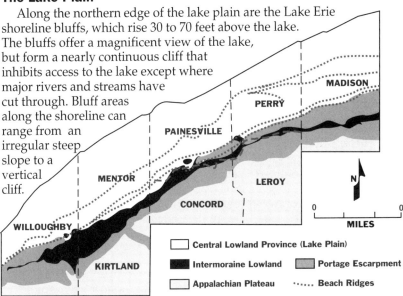

Physiographic regions of Lake County

Access to the lake is easiest at the mouths of the Grand and Chagrin rivers, Red Mill and Arcola creeks and the Mentor Lagoon. The bluffs, composed of loose glacial materials deposited during the Ice Age, are erosion-sensitive and continually changing. Beaches and lakefront properties experience constant battering by wind and water. Erosion control measures are often necessary.

The lake plain is relatively level, but is transversed by a series of old beach ridges running parallel to the current shoreline. They were the shorelines of former glacial lakes which had water levels higher than today's Lake Erie. The

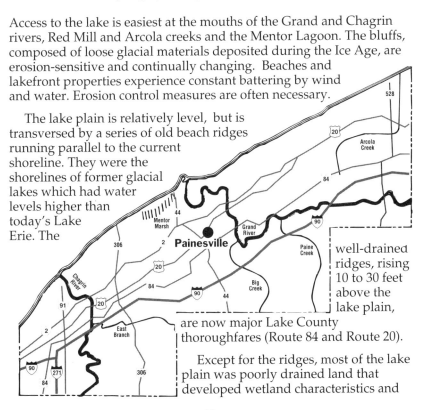

well-drained ridges, rising 10 to 30 feet above the lake plain, are now major Lake County thoroughfares (Route 84 and Route 20).

Except for the ridges, most of the lake plain was poorly drained land that developed wetland characteristics and

7

habitats; however, many of the pristine Lake County wetlands, especially on the west end of the county, have been eliminated by man-made drainage systems.

The level topography of the lake plain makes it attractive for agriculture/horticulture and intensive residential, commercial and industrial development. For conservation and recreation purposes, the most desirable parts of the lake plain are the areas with dramatic natural features such as the lake shore, river or stream valleys, wetlands and ponds.

The Portage Escarpment

The transitional area between the relatively flat lake plain (with a rising elevation of only 100 feet above lake level) and the highlands of the Allegheny Plateau (elevation over 900 feet above lake level) is a rising escarpment, one-to-three miles wide. Referred to as the Portage Escarpment it is the eroded face of the plateau overlaid with glacial deposits.

The Allegheny Plateau

In Lake County, the Allegheny Plateau rises from about 900 feet to 1,247 feet at the top of Little Mountain. Both the escarpment and the plateau are composed of Pennsylvanian and Mississippian Age bedrock and exhibit greater extremes in topography than are found on the lake plain due to the effects of glacial action and erosion on rock formations. Prominences that dominate the landscape, like Little Mountain and Chapin Ledges, are outliers, or caps, of erosion-resistant sandstone conglomerate rock.

Water Features

Water is pivotal to the vitality and appeal of Lake County; even its name tells a part of the story. The surface water features of the county have a strong influence on its visual character and climate, as well as on habitation opportunities for both humans and wildlife. The dominant water features include Lake Erie, major rivers and streams, wetlands and ponds.

Profile of the Great Lakes

Duluth Chicago   St. Marys R. (Soo Locks)
                        Straits of Mackinac

St. Clair River
Lake St. Clair   Cleveland   Welland
Detroit River   Canal

Lake Superior 600 ft. 577 ft.   577 ft.   568 ft.

Lake Michigan

Lake Huron

Lake Erie

St. Lawrence River   +600 ft.

243 ft.

SEA LEVEL

Lake Ontario   0 ft.

Relative Depths

Superior -1329 ft.   Michigan - 922 ft.   Huron - 751 ft.   Erie - 210 ft.   Ontario - 801 ft.

8

Lake Erie

Lake Erie, the shallowest of the five Great Lakes, is a major body of water. The lake reaches 210 feet at its deepest point, but average water depth is 58 feet. It is the most diverse and changeable of the Great Lakes because it is so shallow.

Lake Erie has a significant impact on regional climate, water supply, economic conditions, transportation, recreation, fish and wildlife. The lake is an important environmental and economic asset that has, unfortunately, often been ignored and frequently abused.

Lake County has approximately 30 miles of Lake Erie shoreline and no part of the county is more than 11 miles from the lake shore. All of the rivers and streams that dominate the inland areas of the county flow to Lake Erie. The quality of the lake environment is directly linked to the health of its tributaries and vice versa. A healthy Lake Erie affords a limitless supply of fresh water.

Major River and Stream Watersheds

Lake County is graced with the presence of two out of ten Ohio rivers that are listed in Ohio's Scenic Rivers program. The southern section of the Chagrin River in Kirtland is designated as a state Scenic River. Eastern portions of the Grand River through Painesville meet criteria set by the state for designation as a Wild and Scenic River.

Both the lake plain and the Allegheny Plateau are cut by valleys created by the Grand and Chagrin rivers and several major streams. The Grand River watershed drains 40 percent of Lake County acreage and the Chagrin drains 20 percent.

The Grand River

With roughly 60 percent of Lake County draining into the two watersheds, land use in the county has a direct influence on the water quality of the rivers and Lake Erie. Storm drainage, lawn fertilizers, road salts, oil spills, sewage and other pollutants run off the land and accumulate in the river

The Chagrin River

outlets. The pollutants become concentrated as they are funneled into the waterways headed for Lake Erie. Rivers and streams are critically important to the county and deserve careful attention. Currently, the water quality of the Grand River and the southern portions of the Chagrin River is very good and Lake Erie is experiencing a healthy comeback after decades of problems. When water qualities rebound, the populations and diversity of many fish species may recover within a few years.

The valleys of the major rivers and streams (Big Creek, Paine Creek, Chagrin East Branch, Chagrin Aurora Branch) are characterized by extremes in topography, ranging from flood plains and wetlands to steep ravines and hardwood forests, all critical wildlife habitats. Topographic conditions in many of the valley areas have limited development potential, and these areas remain scenic and pristine, especially the eastern Grand River watershed. Commercial and residential development pressures have heavily affected the Chagrin River watershed in the west end of Lake County.

Water Supply

Within Lake County, water for public, domestic and commercial/industrial use comes from either surface water or ground water. In the cities, industrial and public supplies of water are obtained primarily from Lake Erie. In the eastern portion of the county, local wells in beach ridge deposits and in underlying shale and sandstone bedrock produce water for domestic use and irrigation. Lake County wells range in depth from five to 200 feet. Well-water drillers commonly strike sulfur water or brine when deep-drilling through shale bedrock.

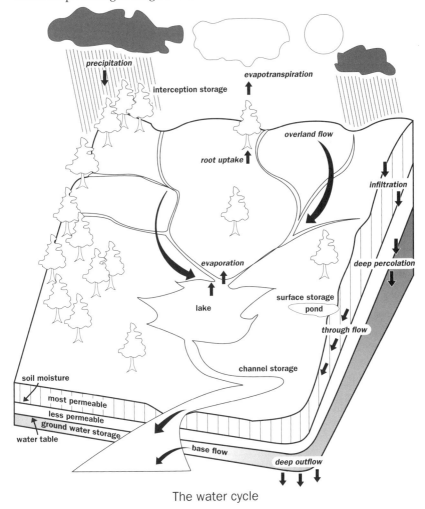

The water cycle

Groundwater reserves are very low for most of Lake County with average yields ranging from one to three GPM (gallons per minute). A typical household usually requires three to ten GPM. Some wells that are drilled into the sand and gravel of the East branch of the Chagrin River flood plain may produce water at rates up to 25 GPM.

Lake County has been mapping its ground water systems for pollution potential in order to monitor and prevent contamination of ground water resources.

Soils

Lake County soils reflect the effects of glacial action. The last series of glaciers deposited tills, unsorted mixtures of scraped bedrock, clay, silt, sand and pebbles, in identifiable sheets throughout northeastern Ohio. One or more layers of the tills covered much of the Allegheny Plateau. In most of Lake County, the till is scattered and rarely more than 20 feet thick. Two exceptions are found on the Portage Escarpment, the prominent Euclid and Painesville Moraines, where the till is as much as 100 feet thick.

Representative Lake County soils

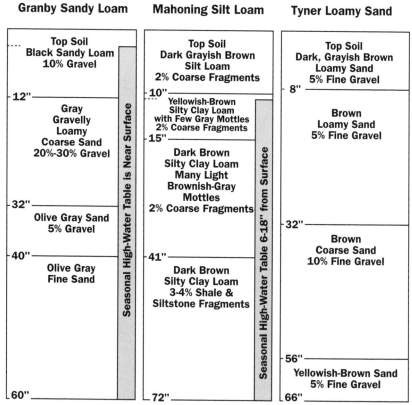

Granby Sandy Loam

Top Soil
Black Sandy Loam
10% Gravel
12"
Gray Gravelly Loamy Coarse Sand 20%-30% Gravel
32"
Olive Gray Sand 5% Gravel
40"
Olive Gray Fine Sand
60"

Seasonal High-Water Table is Near Surface

Mahoning Silt Loam

Top Soil
Dark Grayish Brown Silt Loam
2% Coarse Fragments
10"
Yellowish-Brown Silty Clay Loam with Few Gray Mottles 2% Coarse Fragments
15"
Dark Brown Silty Clay Loam Many Light Brownish-Gray Mottles 2% Coarse Fragments
41"
Dark Brown Silty Clay Loam 3-4% Shale & Siltstone Fragments
72"

Seasonal High-Water Table 6-18" from Surface

Tyner Loamy Sand

Top Soil
Dark, Grayish Brown Loamy Sand 5% Fine Gravel
8"
Brown Loamy Sand 5% Fine Gravel
32"
Brown Coarse Sand 10% Fine Gravel
56"
Yellowish-Brown Sand 5% Fine Gravel
66"

Granby Sandy Loam: Very poorly drained, rapidly permeable soil formed in sandy glaciofluvial soils on basin-like depressions on the lake plain.

Mahoning Silt Loam: Somewhat poorly drained, slowly permeable soil formed on glacial till plains.

Tyner Loamy Sand: Well drained soil formed on upper parts of post-glacial beach ridges, rapidly permeable.

The lake plain is covered primarily by silt and sand deposits of the late-glacial and post-glacial lakes that also left behind the sandy, gravely old beach ridges. Lake plain soils provide excellent conditions for horticultural nurseries to flourish in Lake County.

Rich alluvial deposits of sand and silt are also present along the flood plain of major rivers and streams and on the high terraces that were formerly flood plain.

The parent soils are modified into locally unique soils by the complex interaction of several soil-forming factors including land slope, drainage, climate, and plant, animal and microbial life.

Climate

Lake County's climate is humid-continental in character with warm summers and cold winters. The growing season averages 165 days. Precipitation is well distributed throughout the year and is adequate for most cultivated crops. During the day, average relative humidity is about 60 percent. Humidity is higher at night in all seasons, and the average at dawn is about 80 percent. The probability of sunshine is 70 percent in summer and 30 percent in winter. Prevailing wind direction is from the west and the average wind speed is highest in March.

The topography of the county and the position of Lake Erie greatly affect climatic conditions, especially in winter. The lake plain and the Allegheny Plateau run parallel in a northeasterly direction. High-pressure systems, with characteristically strong winds, move across Lake Erie from the northwest. As a result, Lake Erie significantly influences the Lake County climate in three ways: increased lake-effect snowfall, lake breeze air temperature variations, and extended growing season.

Lake-Effect Snow

Lake-effect snowstorms occur downwind of a large body of open water when the air temperature is cold enough to form snow and the open water temperature is above freezing. Lake Erie cools down more slowly than the land in the late fall. A mass of cold, high-pressure air,

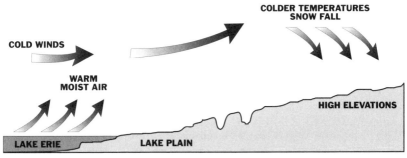

Conditions that produce lake-effect snowfall

an "Alberta Clipper," coming out of Canada, can quickly drop moderate air temperature to as low as 10 to 25 degrees Fahrenheit. With Lake Erie surface temperatures at approximately 50 degrees F., a convection current of moisture-laden air from the warmer lake moves upward. The moist air rises into the upper-flowing colder air, causing the water vapor to condense into clouds and precipitate in the form of snow. The snowfall is increased in areas where topography, lake orientation, and the direction of high-pressure systems cause additional uplifting and cooling as the

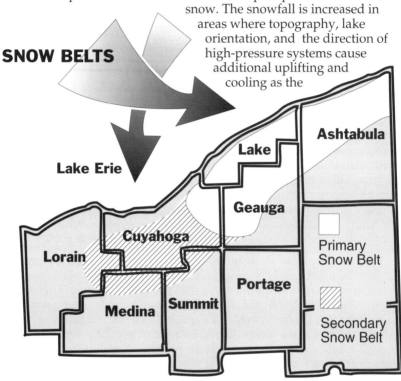

moist, unstable air moves onshore. Regions where this lake-effect snow is common are referred to as snowbelts.

With the lake plain at approximately 600 feet elevation and the Plateau highlands at about 1100 feet elevation, on a northeast/southwest axis, Lake County is a prime region for lake-effect snow.

The Lake Erie snowbelt extends from the eastern suburbs of Cleveland to Buffalo, NY. in narrow bands from five to 15 miles wide. Within these belts, blizzard-like conditions prevail with near-zero visibility and snow rapidly accumulates six to 12 inches within hours. Outside the snowbelt, conditions may be relatively clear. The highlands of the Little Mountain vicinity in Kirtland and the Chardon area in Geauga County annually receive nearly twice as much snow as communities on the lake plain. Average seasonal snowfall in Lake County is among the highest to be found this far south in North America.

Lake Breeze Influence

The lake breeze modifies temperatures up to three miles inland along the lake plain. The breeze may cool the lakefront area as much as five to ten degrees F. during the day and maintain warmer night-time temperatures by the same extent compared to the inland high ground areas. Thus, daily temperature fluctuations on the lake plain are less exaggerated due to the lake breeze influence.

Extended Growing Season

Lake Erie has a generally modifying effect on temperature changes and frost dates. Early in the growing season, crop development is slowed by the frequent, cool winds blowing over a cold lake. This slowing is important for fruit crops that generally do not blossom until after the chance of a spring freeze passes. The townships bordering the lake have their last spring frosts from ten to twenty days sooner than do the southern townships and a similar delay in fall frosts. Winds that blow off a relatively warm lake delay the first freeze in fall and prolong the growing season for all crops.

The overall seasonal effect is the lengthening of the growing season on the lake plain by at least three weeks, making it a prime horticultural and vineyard area within Lake County. The average growing season along the lake is 178 days; in Concord and Leroy townships, the average growing season is 150 days.

Lake plain nurseries

The Shape of the Land

Hundreds of millions of years ago powerful geological forces set Lake County bedrock in place. A few million years ago, the glaciers of the Ice Age began sculpting dramatic changes across northern Ohio and created many of the distinctive features of today's Lake County landscape.

Understanding the geology of a region is the first step in understanding its natural history. Rocks set the stage for the rest of the story: geology influences not only the shape of the land, but affects climate, soils, vegetation, habitats and even human activity.

This brief overview of Lake County's bedrock begins with the massive layers of unseen rocks buried deep beneath the county and progresses through to the layers of rock and sediment visible at the surface.

Subsurface Bedrock

Some 6,000 plus feet beneath the surface rock layers of Lake County are the foundation or "basement" rocks. They extend downward for miles. These metamorphic rocks, a billion or so years old, were created

Geologic

Era	Cenozoic		Mesozoic			Paleozoic	
Period	Quaternary	Tertiary	Cretaceous	Jurassic	Triassic	Permian	Pennsylvanian
Millions of Years Ago		2	65	145	205	245	285

☐ No representation in Lake Co.

North

Unseen Bedrock in Lake County

Lake

Salina Group (Silurian)
Niagaran Series (Sil.)
Clinton Formation (Sil.)
Ordovician Rocks
Medina Sandstone (Sil.)

Profile of subsurface and surface rock layers in Lake County

16

from pre-existing rocks altered by heat and pressure during Precambrian time. Occasionally, Lake County is subject to powerful earthquakes that originate within these Precambrian Age rocks. A prime example occurred in 1986 when an earthquake with a magnitude of about 5.0 on the Richter Scale was centered approximately six miles below the surface of southeastern Painesville.

Above the Precambrian rock layers is a thick series of subsurface sedimentary rocks deposited during the Paleozoic Era. The most familiar subsurface rocks are the salt layers which belong to the Salina Group. This group includes sequences of bedded salt, dolomite, shale, and anhydrite.

At the Fairport Harbor mine, the salt deposits are located in three zones, 1900 to 2400 feet below the surface. The salt beds were formed about 410 million years ago, during the Silurian Period. At that time, the continental plate containing portions of what is now North America was positioned in the tropics. Fossils of calcareous (limey) algae found in the Salina Group indicate that the salt formed in, or very near, a shallow marine environment. The layers were created by the evaporation of vast amounts of sea water.

Time Table

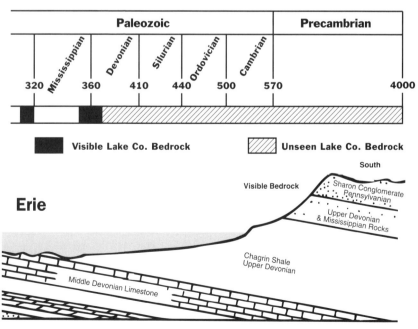

	Paleozoic					Precambrian
320	Mississippian	Devonian	Silurian	Ordovician	Cambrian	
	360	410	440	500	570	4000

■ Visible Lake Co. Bedrock   ▨ Unseen Lake Co. Bedrock

Erie

South

Visible Bedrock

Sharon Conglomerate
Pennsylvanian

Upper Devonian
& Mississippian Rocks

Chagrin Shale
Upper Devonian

Middle Devonian Limestone

Salt "rooms" in the mines beneath Lake Erie

Salt is mined commercially from beneath Lake Erie at Fairport Harbor by the "room and pillar" method. This method removes deposits in solid form. Huge roomfuls of rock salt, or halite, are excavated, leaving massive pillars between rooms to support the mine ceiling. Rock salt is used primarily for snow and ice removal and has also been used as an important ingredient in a variety of industrial and chemical operations. "Wet" mining, in which water is pumped into the salt and the salt is returned to the surface dissolved in a brine solution, is another means of salt retrieval. However, this method was abandoned in Lake County by the mid-1970s.

Other notable subsurface rocks are those of Silurian and Devonian Age in which oil and gas pools occur. In the past, gas was obtained from shallow wells drilled into the Devonian shales. Today the best-producing rocks are the deeper rocks located more than 3100 feet below the surface: Oriskany Sandstone, Newburg Dolomite, and Clinton Sandstone. In the Madison Township area, the rocks, primarily Clinton Sandstone, range from 1600 to 2800 feet thick. The oil and gas are contained in pore spaces between grains of rock.

Beyond their commercial value, deep and ancient rocks hold clues to understanding the powerful and dynamic forces that formed and continually reshape the surface of the earth.

Surface Rocks

Stacked on top of the deep, unseen subsurface rocks are the exposed sedimentary rock layers formed during the middle and late parts of the Paleozoic Era when the Lake County region was often covered by seas. Mud, silt and sand were deposited as sea levels fluctuated. Gradually, the layers of sediment solidified into layers of shale, siltstone and sandstone.

Surface Bedrock Layers

ERA	AGE	ROCK UNIT		SECTION
Cenozoic	Quaternary	Glacial Deposits (Probably less than 20,000 years old)		
PALEOZOIC (Paleozoic rocks in Lake County are between 360 and 300 million years old)	Penn-sylvanian	Sharon Conglomerate		
	Mississippian	Cuyahoga Group	Sharpsville Formation	
			Orangeville Formation	
		Berea Sandstone		
	?	Bedford Formation		
		Cleveland Shale		
	Devonian	Chagrin Shale		

 Crossbeds

 Sandstone

 Black Shale

 Conglomerate

 Siltstone

 Gray Shale

19

Exposed rock formations are easy to locate and identify at any time of the year. They offer even the most casual observer the opportunity to examine materials that are millions of years old. The distribution of bedrock found at the surface throughout Lake County was first recorded in detail by geologist Michael C. Read in an 1873 Ohio Geological Survey report. Accompanying his report was a map showing the major rock layers. Since this classic work, a number of geologists have provided additional information about these rocks and the prehistoric environments in which they were formed.

Penitentiary Glen gorge

The best views of surface bedrock are seen along natural bluffs, stream valleys and road cuts. There is no single easily accessible place in Lake County where all the layers of exposed bedrock can be viewed together. However, a major section of the sequence, from the top of the Chagrin Shale through the Berea Sandstone, can been seen along Stoney Brook in the Lake Metropark Penitentiary Glen Reservation east of State Route 306 on Kirtland Chardon Road.

Brachiopods like this rhynchonellid are the most commonly preserved body fossils found in Chagrin Shale. The three-fourth-inch specimen, above, was collected along Mill Creek.

Chagrin Shale

The great gray cliffs found in the northern and middle sections of Lake County are composed primarily of shales, (fossilized mud), with alternating layers of fine-grained siltstone. The edges of the siltstone tend to jut out from the cliffs because the shales are soft and more easily eroded than are the harder siltstone layers.

The shale and siltstone are a part of the rock unit known as Chagrin Shale, at one time referred to as Erie Shale. Chagrin Shale is the lowermost and oldest rock unit exposed in Lake County. Exposed outcrops represent only a portion of the total thickness of Chagrin Shale, which covers more of Lake County than any other rock unit. Chagrin Shale is actually a great wedge of gray shale. Most of it is beneath the surface, underlying the northern lake plain region of the county, widening toward the east. In Perry Township, Chagrin Shale is about 750 feet thick. Spectacular outcrops can be found at various spots along Interstate 90 and in the Lake Metropark Hidden Valley and Hell Hollow Reservations. Less dramatic examples are abundant along many smaller streams in the northern two-thirds of Lake County.

At first glance, Chagrin Shale appears rather uniform; but, this rock unit is really quite variable. Much of the variation occurs in the thickness and spacing of the siltstone beds that protrude from the cliffs. The gray shales and siltstones were deposited as sea-bottom muds and silts toward the end of the Devonian Period, about 360 million years ago. At that time, seas covering this area were relatively shallow, less than 1000 feet deep at their deepest point.

The sediments were probably laid down in waters less than 300 feet deep along the shores of the Old Red Sandstone Continent, an ancient, huge, land mass that contained parts of what are now continental Europe, Great Britain, and North America. The western shorelines of the old continent extended to central Pennsylvania. Muds accumulated slowly on the sea bottom when the seas were quiet. During periodic storms, silts washed off the land mass and settled on the sea floor. Additional muds settled above these silt layers. Over time, this resulted in alternating layers of muds and silts. Eventually the mud particles were compressed and transformed into clay minerals. The minerals solidified into shales, and the layers of silts were cemented into hard layers of siltstone.

Eroded outcrops of Chagrin Shale with resistant caps of siltstone form many of Lake County's scenic waterfalls, including Paine Falls. Sharp, distinctive shale ridges, called razorbacks, are frequently seen along streams where Chagrin Shale outcrops have eroded. Excellent examples of razorbacks can be found at Penitentiary Glen Reservation.

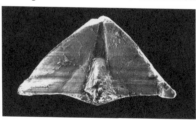

The triangular shape of the brachiopod *Sphenospira* is quite distinctive. This specimen found in Chagrin Shale in Madison Twp. is two-and-one-quarter inches across.

Chagrin Shale contains the fossil remains of clams, snails, crustaceans and other animals. The most frequently found fossils are brachiopods, prehistoric, shelled, marine invertebrates that superficially resemble clams. Trace fossils, including trackways, burrows and other features resulting from the movement of prehistoric marine animals, are more common than body fossils in Chagrin Shale. The fossil organisms and trackways that are found in the Chagrin Shale indicate that the surface of the mud was fairly soft and that the portion of the water column near the sea bottom contained less oxygen than normal sea water.

The Chagrin Shale yields some gas. Natural gas seeps or springs have long been known in the county and were once found along the Grand River and on the banks of the Chagrin River in Willoughby. In the past, the Chagrin Shale was a target for commercial drillers, but the amount of gas produced was relatively small.

Cleveland Shale

Rocks that occur above the Chagrin Shale can best be seen at higher elevations on the Portage Escarpment, which forms the boundary between the lake plain and the glaciated Allegheny Plateau.

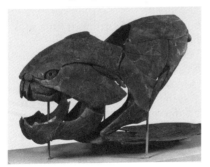

Dunkleosteus - A giant armored fish fossil found in Cleveland Shale

Directly above the Chagrin Shale is a layer of black shale, ranging up to 35 feet in thickness, with a typically blocky appearance. This is Cleveland Shale, another Late Devonian Age rock unit.

The black color of the shale is not always obvious when looking at a weathered outcrop, but breaking open a small piece of the shale will reveal its unweathered color. A high content of organic materials produces the dark color.

Cleveland Shale is composed of rocks that originated as bottom muds in a deeper part of the sea. Fossils are scarce in Cleveland Shale, however, it is famous for its fossil fish, which are found primarily in Cuyahoga County where this layer is the thickest. The scarcity of fossils in Lake County and the mode of preservation of the fossil fish in Cuyahoga County indicate very oxygen-poor conditions in the bottom waters.

Bedford Formation

The gray shales and siltstones of the Bedford Formation lie above the Cleveland Shale. Determining the boundary between the Cleveland and the Bedford Formation is difficult because the two rock units often grade into one another. The Bedford Formation can reach 70 feet in thickness in Lake County, but is often thinner. Some of the best exposures of the Bedford Formation are those at Penitentiary Glen Reservation, but the upper part of the unit can also be seen at Chapin Forest Reservation off State Route 306. Rocks of the Bedford Formation originated as offshore deposits, or possibly, lagoonal muds. It is a shallower-water formation than Cleveland Shale. The Bedford Formation contains some trace fossils and occasional remnants of shelled organisms.

The thicker siltstone layers in the Bedford Formation often form the setting for small waterfalls. Interesting folds occur within the formation. These appear to have been created by the movement of sediment shortly after it was laid down and still soft but before it solidified completely.

Berea Sandstone

Berea Sandstone is found above the Bedford Formation. The thickness of the Berea varies considerably, ranging between 30 and 70 feet in Lake County. The sands that comprise Berea Sandstone were deposited along the margins of the Old Red Continent's shoreline during the early part of the Mississippian

Quarry cut at Chapin Ledges

Period, about 350 million years ago. Sands accumulated on and offshore as river deposits, delta lobes and as offshore bodies of sand.

Ripple marks, alternating ridges and troughs created by wave action, are prominent in the Berea Sandstone, as are crossbeds. Crossbeds are sedimentary layers that run at an angle to normal horizontal bedding. They indicate the direction of water currents at the time the sandy layers were deposited. Because Berea Sandstone is a hard stone and more resistant to erosion than the underlying softer shale of the Bedford Formation, it often forms the top lip of scenic waterfalls.

The Kirtland RLDS Temple on Chillicothe Road was built with local sandstone

Berea Sandstone, once called Berea grit, was used extensively for grindstones and as a building material. Quarry Lake in Chapin Forest Reservation, the site of an early Berea Sandstone quarry, may have been the source of stone used for the Kirtland RLDS Temple on Chillicothe Road. Most of the stone used for the Temple however, is covered by stucco. Berea Sandstone was also commercially quarried in southern Concord Township.

23

Cuyahoga Group

The Cuyahoga Group, which overlies the Berea Sandstone is also Mississippian in age. This rock group reaches a thickness of approximately 180 feet within Lake County. Rocks of the Cuyahoga layer include a shaly unit, the Orangeville Formation, and a shaly-to-sandy unit, called the Sharpsville Formation. Rocks of the Cuyahoga Group are typically covered by glacial debris, soil and vegetation, so are seldom seen in Lake County. A few outcrops are found along Bates and Phelps creeks in Leroy Township in the southeastern portion of the county.

An outcropping of Sharon Conglomerate

Sharon Conglomerate

Among the most striking natural features in Lake County are the massive cliffs known in northeastern Ohio as "ledges". These cliffs are composed of outcrops of Sharon Conglomerate, a pebbly sandstone of the Pennsylvanian Age. A time gap of perhaps 30 million years elapsed before the Sharon Conglomerate was deposited over extensively eroded portions of the Cuyahoga Formation.

Sharon Conglomerate is the youngest bedrock in Lake County and occurs only in a few places as outliers or caps of hills. The Sharon varies in thickness, but is usually about 50 feet thick. Little Mountain, the highest point in Lake County, and nearby smaller hills to the south and east, are capped by layers of Sharon Conglomerate. The Holden Arboretum provides guided hikes to Little Mountain.

Some of the most accessible outcrops of Sharon Conglomerate in Lake County are found in the Lake Metropark Chapin Forest Reservation. A hike through the higher elevations of Chapin Forest, along formerly quarried areas, reveals several beautiful exposures of the conglomerate.

The characteristic rounded, white quartz pebbles of Sharon Conglomerate are known locally as "lucky stones." These pebbles are sometimes quite abundant. Such massive quantities of quartz pebbles

Quartz "lucky stones" erode out from Sharon Conglomerate

had to originate in a quartz-rich source. The most likely source is Canada, where crystalline rocks could have eroded from igneous deposits. Studies of northeastern Ohio outcrops of Sharon Conglomerate indicate that large, criss-crossing streams brought the sand and pebbles from the north.

Because the underlying rocks of the Cuyahoga Group are soft and easily eroded, massive blocks of the conglomerate often break off at the edge of the rock ledges. A few of the more dramatic chunks are given names like "Pulpit Rock." Settling causes cracks, fissures and large cave-like crevices to develop in the Sharon.

Sharon Conglomerate has long been quarried in Lake County. During the 19th century, oxen were used to haul quarry stone and many small bridges were built with the sturdy conglomerate. The Doty Road Bridge over Mill Creek is a prime example. Until the 1970s, the northern ledges of Chapin Forest were a commercial quarry site.

During the Ages of Dinosaurs

Lake County does not contain any rocks dating from the vast time span comprising the Mesozoic Era (about 245 - 65 million years ago) and most of the Cenozoic Era (about 65 million years ago to the present). The Lake County region was most likely a hilly upland area during the Mesozoic Era when dinosaurs roamed the earth, so hunting for their remains in Lake County would be futile. Any sediment of the Mesozoic and Cenozoic ages that may have been deposited has eroded without a trace. During the last part of the Cenozoic Era, a river system ran along what is now the Great Lakes. One section of the old system, a stream sometimes referred to as the Erigan River, ran closely along what is now the long axis of Lake Erie. Glaciers profoundly changed that river system and the face of Ohio.

The Impact of the Ice Age

Several episodes of cooling occurred from about 1.6 million years ago to about 10,000 years ago. During this geologic epoch known as the Pleistocene, or Ice Age, compacted snow formed a succession of massive glaciers that periodically advanced and retreated over portions of Ohio including Lake County. The moving glaciers scoured the land and dragged deposits of sand, clay, gravel and boulders over exposed bedrock and into lowland areas.

Glaciers, like this one in Alaska, once covered Lake County

During the last period of glacial action, which occurred between 23,000 and 14,500 years ago, all of northeastern Ohio was at times beneath a frozen mass. Glacial ice moves slowly and follows a course of least resistance. Initially, the glaciers moved along the lowlands and around high ground. But, at the peak of major advances, even the conglomerate-topped highlands of Lake County were covered. It is estimated that at one time as much as a mile-thick layer of ice covered northeastern Ohio. Each new glacial advance obscured most of the record of the previous advance. Scratches made by boulders and rocks being dragged along by the ice can be seen on some of the outcrops of Sharon Conglomerate in Lake County.

Glacial Lakes

Glaciers had an enormous impact on water drainage patterns. Frequently, stream outlets blocked by ice caused lowland flooding, especially south of the ice mass. Between 14,500 and 12,500 years ago, the last glacier began melting back to the north and water levels in the Erie Basin changed several times, forming a series of high water lakes that preceded the present Lake Erie.

Ancient Beach Ridges

Each time the basin waters receded, silt and fine sand filtered out and settled. Sand bars, beaches, and dune fields formed along the shoreline. A series of beach ridges, some with fossil dunes, still remain to mark the ancient lake shores.

Lake County is crossed by five major remnant beach ridges that run parallel to the current lake shore. Each one is named for the ancient lake it represents: the Maumee II, the Whittlesey, the Arkona, the Warren, and the Elkton. The ridges vary in width, but are typically between one-tenth to one-half a mile.

Two of the ridges are distinctive features running midway through Lake County. To the south, the highly prominent ridge, with an elevation of 740 to 750 feet, is the Whittlesey Ridge also known as the South Ridge. This ridge, marking the shoreline of glacial Lake Whittlesey, runs very close to Route 84 and is the approximate boundary between the lake plain and the Portage Escarpment. To the north, between the Whittlesey Ridge and the Lake Erie shoreline is the Lake Warren Ridge which runs along Route 20. The well-drained sandy ridges became natural east-west travel routes for Native Americans and early settlers. Since then the ridges have become Lake County's major thoroughfares.

Glacial Deposits

Glaciers often filled pre-glacial valleys and stream beds with a clay-silt-gravel mixture. Rivers coursing in, under and on top of the ice mass carried boulders and other debris. As the glacier receded, the

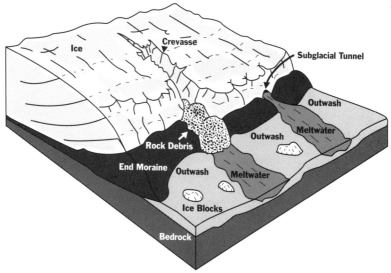

Glacial action alters land features

27

loose materials, now referred to as tills, were simply dropped and left behind. When the southern edge of the glaciers melted back, a thick accumulation of material marked the edge position. The mounds of debris formed a series of broad ridges called terminal or end moraines. Two major end moraines cross Lake County. Both run along the Portage Escarpment at the edge of the highlands. These end moraines are extensive and range from 1/4 of a mile to two miles in width. The higher, more southerly deposit is the Euclid Moraine; to the north and slightly smaller is the Painesville Moraine. A lowland area, transversed in part by the Grand River, separates the two. End moraine tills can be as much as 100 feet thick and are laid down in distinctive layers that identify the period of glacial advance.

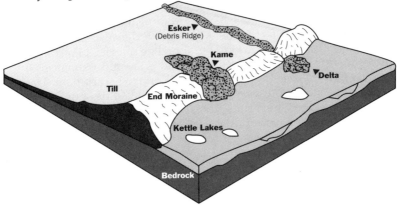

Land features after glacial retreat

Most of the higher elevations within Lake County are covered with silts, clay and other deposits. These glacial tills are rarely more than 20 feet thick and erode easily.

In some of the swampy, low-lying areas on the lake plain, iron deposits accumulated over the past 10,000 years since the end of the Ice Age creating pockets of bog iron that had commercial value to early Lake County settlers.

Erie Basin

Water levels in the Erie Basin changed dramatically about 12,500 years ago. The weight of the last ice mass depressed the eastern Niagara Basin so much that the Erie Basin waters and other waters to the north rushed eastward in a raging flood. Erie Basin water levels dropped significantly and remained low for several thousand years. Gradually, between 7,000 and 5,000 years ago, northern lake waters were forced south and formed Lake Erie at its current level.

Post-Glacial Vegetation

The variety of vegetation found throughout Lake County today is tied to the complex changes that resulted from the glaciation of the landscape. Glacial action precipitated the conditions for a succession of plant communities that would eventually lead to present day patterns.

When the last glacier slowly retreated from the Lake County region, plant species began to colonize on exposed bedrock, glacial deposits and lake bottom sediments. As the ice melted, tundra vegetation, composed largely of moss and lichens adapted to cold conditions, most likely was the first to become established. A number of specialized plant communities followed in response to ever-changing moisture, soil, light and air temperature conditions.

New vegetation and wildlife appeared in northeastern Ohio
after the last ice mass retreated

Soil development was minimal for several hundred years. Between 13,000 and 12,000 years ago, the tundra vegetation was replaced by a spruce-fir forest community. Root growth and soil animals began to break up and aerate the compacted glacial till. Water moved downward through the soil carrying minerals, clay and silt to the lower layers. Approximately 10,000 years ago, the glacial margin retreated rapidly north as the warming trend continued. The cold-tolerant spruce-fir forest declined. Pine forests briefly dotted the warming landscape until oxygen penetrated deeper into the soil, setting up conditions for deciduous trees to move into the region.

Patterns of Vegetation

About 10,000 years ago, when cold-tolerant vegetation declined as air temperatures rose, many of the deciduous tree species that dominate Ohio today migrated from the south and became established. Water drainage patterns, soil development and light conditions ultimately determined which tree species and plant communities would thrive in Lake County after the post-glacial warming.

Slow-growing beech-maple forests flourish on upland terrain. The hemlock-hardwood association, typical of the higher elevations in the east and in Canada, find suitable conditions on the cool slopes of deep ravines in the south-southeastern portions of the county. The chestnut-oak association is usually seen along the drier ridges of the river valleys and on outcrops of sandstone. Fast-growing broadleaf tree species which can tolerate mixed conditions form the forests of river valley terraces, and trees that thrive in poor drainage conditions become the swamp forest associations of the wetlands.

The pioneers in this photo are dwarfed by trees of the virgin forest

Today's Landscape

Until two hundred years ago, northeastern Ohio was approximately 98% forested. The remaining 2% of surface land was in small open areas: freshwater marshes, bogs, prairies and occasional open oak savannahs on the beach ridges and river flood plains.

Today, vegetation in Lake County is considerably different from that encountered by early pioneers. At first, the immensity of the primeval forest was intimidating to the settlers, but within decades they would irrevocably alter the range of the forest and change the face of the landscape. While Native Americans made slight modifications for raising crops, European and eastern settlers converted vast acres of forest into agricultural fields. They dammed streams and drained wetlands. The changes were monumental.

Settlers also caused a less perceptible, but major impact on the environment by introducing non-native plants into northeastern Ohio. A majority of plants found in Lake County today are non-native species. The large number of native plant communities covering the county until a few hundred years ago has dwindled dramatically. Only a few pristine examples of the original plant communities can be found within Lake County today.

The plants and wildlife of the southern, scenic highlands of Lake County and the immediate Lake Erie shoreline have always been well documented, but little was known about the plant communities and ecosystems of the wetlands and the beach ridges of the lake plain. Recent studies reveal the significance of these areas and the scope of their decline. Wetlands serve as important indicators of the health of the general environment.

Shoreline and Wetlands Plant Communities

Lake Erie strongly influences the climatic conditions and vegetation patterns found within Lake County. Along the shoreline, particular conditions are present for specialized and sensitive plant communities to develop: sand and dune habitats, marshes, and river mouth wetlands.

Beach Ridges and "Fossil" Sand Dunes

Near the end of the Ice Age, the water level of the glacial lakes was higher than present Lake Erie levels and covered more of the lake plain region. The series of ancient beach ridges left behind as markers of that age are an important resource for understanding post-glacial vegetation. Some of the best examples of well-developed fossil dune deposits are in Perry and Madison Townships.

Recent studies of the plants on the ridges offer insights about species native to Ohio that are rare today, such as wild lupine and racemed milkwort. These species, found on sand barrens and oak savannahs, probably thrived on the old dune surfaces in Lake County. The fossil dunes found along the old beach ridges are rapidly vanishing because they are prime sites for development. Unless these areas are protected, study of the best of these old dune surfaces may no longer be possible and an important historical record of Lake County's natural heritage may be lost.

Lake Plain Wetlands - The Swamp Forest

Most of the land between the old ridges and the current Lake Erie bluff is level and poorly drained ground. The soil is composed primarily of lake bottom sediments, fine textured clays and silts interspersed with sandy deposits which were left behind thousands of years ago each time the glacial lakes drained back. Much of northern Lake County was swampy and covered by large tracts of swamp forest until draining of the area by settlers began 200 years ago.

The dominant species of the original mature swamp forest was an elm-ash-maple plant community with an abundance of white elm (American elm), red, black and pumpkin ash, and early blooming red and/or silver maple.

31

A swamp forest

Recently, studies of the remnants of the old swamp forest in Lake County done by The Cleveland Museum of Natural History revealed that a great variety of other trees existed in the canopy. For example, pumpkin ash, not previously reported in this region, was found to occur frequently within the lake plain swamps of Lake County. In some areas, the diversity in the canopy and understory approaches that of a mixed mesophytic forest - the transitional, broadleaf, hardwood forest - usually found in areas with balanced drainage rather than swampy lands.

The variety of tree species in the swamp forest canopy is a result of the wind-throw phenomenon, which creates conditions for a "hummock/hollow" woods. Trees in high-water, swampy areas tend to have very shallow roots and are vulnerable in high winds. When a tree blows over, the exposed root ball decomposes and forms a small rise on the forest floor known as a hummock. A hollow occurs in the ground that the root ball occupied and the new depression soon fills with water to form a pool within the forest. Gaps in the canopy following the frequent blow-down of trees increase the amount of light that can filter to the ground. In turn this permits intermediate, shade-tolerant, mixed broadleaf trees to invade the midst of the elm/ash/maple forest by seeding themselves on the better-lit decomposing root balls. Tulip, cherry, beech, cucumber magnolia, sassafras, yellow birch, tupelo, shagbark and bitternut hickories, and black walnut can often be found in the hummock-hollow swamp forest.

Swamp forest wildflower understory

A broad spectrum of wildflowers and ferns flourish on the swamp forest floor. Ginseng, wild geranium, mayflower, trillium, and hepatica are some of the wildflower species that thrive.

The large, root-ball hollows fill with water in the spring and serve as springtime breeding habitats for unusual amphibians such as the mole salamander, the four-toed salamander and the wood frog, as well as the more familiar spring peepers.

Not much remains of the old swamp forest today except a few protected examples at Veterans Memorial Park in Mentor and in undeveloped areas in eastern Madison Township north of U.S. Route 20. Swamp forests also occurred south of the lake plain on poorly drained lowland regions between the two glacial end moraines, the Euclid Moraine and the Painesville Moraine. East of State Route 306, Interstate 90 crosses over some of this intermoraine wetland. Intermorainal wetland forests appear to be similar to the lake plain hummock-hollow forests.

Spring peeper

Most of Lake County's extensive wetland areas have been drained and built upon. Drainage disrupts the delicately balanced conditions that support a swamp forest habitat.

River-Mouth Wetlands

Some of the most spectacular natural communities in Lake County occur along the shoreline where rivers and creeks enter Lake Erie. Fluctuating water levels, short and long term, create conditions for the specialized wetland plant communities found in open beach areas, emergent marshes, palustrine sand plains, aquatic beds, shrub swamps and swamp forests.

The intriguing habitats located at the mouths of streams entering Lake Erie are linked to the

Arrowhead

movement of shoreline waves that continually deposit and rearrange sand at the lake's edge. Through the dynamics of wave action, sand is carried from west to east along the beach shelf. This process, known as littoral drift, builds deposits of sand on the western side of a river mouth entering Lake Erie.

Pickerel weed

Wave action has been known to build sand spits that extend all the way across a river channel. A sand spit blocks normal drainage and permits ideal conditions for the development of marshes and estuaries. A close look at the river mouths along the shores of Lake Erie in Lake County reveals that impressive wetlands tend to form upstream of a blocked river outlet.

In the past, huge volumes of sand would collect at the mouths of the Grand and Chagrin Rivers, Arcola Creek and the western end of Mentor Marsh. The Grand River mouth was the site of massive sand spit formations before the channel was dredged and breakwalls and jetties were constructed to protect Fairport Harbor.

Prior to the construction of the jetty for the Eastlake power plant in the early 1950s, summer accumulations of sand routinely blocked the mouth of the Chagrin River and, according to local residents, it was possible to walk from bank to bank on the sand spit.

Sand Spit and Dune Vegetation

When a breakwall is present, sand tends to build out into the lake along the western edge of the wall. Breakwalls erected in the 19th century began to alter the natural littoral drift wave action. Less sand moved into and across the mouths of the rivers, and more sand was deposited on the beach. This process

Lake Erie

Breakwalls

Shorelines 1975 1937

Jetties

Fairport

1876

1826

N

0   1/2   1
Miles

0   1/2   1
Kilometers

Expansion of Headlands Beach area

occurred at what is now Mentor Headlands, creating an extensive beach and well-formed sand dunes. The process, as well as the dunes and the accompanying native dune plant species, can be observed at the Mentor Headlands State Nature Preserve.

Sand dunes at Mentor Headlands State Nature Preserve

American beach grass and coastal little bluestem are the dominant dune builders at Mentor Headlands Beach. Two other grasses that occur there, switch grass and Canada wild rye, are the important dune builders at the other beaches in Lake County.

Atlantic coastal dune plants, such as those typical of Cape Cod and other east coast sand beaches, are now found on the best sand spits in northern Lake County. Beach pea occurs at Mentor Headlands Beach, Lakeshore Reservation, on the open sands at the mouth of the Chagrin River, and the sand spit along the mouth of Arcola Creek. Other coastal species found in the dune-building sands at the river mouths are sea rocket, seaside spurge and purple sand grass.

Palustrine Sand Plain

Behind the first line of dunes at Mentor Headlands Beach are the recently restored wet sandy flats known as palustrine sand plains, also called the pan or interdunal wetlands. The palustrine sand plain community is sparse and transitory, coming and going rapidly in response to lake water levels.

When the lake level is high, the dry sand flats between the dunes become palustrine (swamplike) and covered with wetland plant

Palustrine sand plain behind Headlands dunes

species. Typical among palustrine species are many grass-like plants including rushes, sedges and bulrushes. Alpine rush is very common and silver weed appears. This habitat often supports rare plants.

When the lake level falls, the process is reversed and the palustrine sand plain community moves down slope onto newly exposed beach flats. Seeds of the palustrine sand species apparently are stored within the dry sands during periods of low water levels.

Historically, the best palustrine sand plain in Lake County probably occurred at the western end of Mentor Marsh, the mouth of the Grand River, and the mouth of the Chagrin River. Today, a good example of the palustrine sand plain plant community can be found along the shores of Granger Pond at Veterans Memorial Park in Mentor.

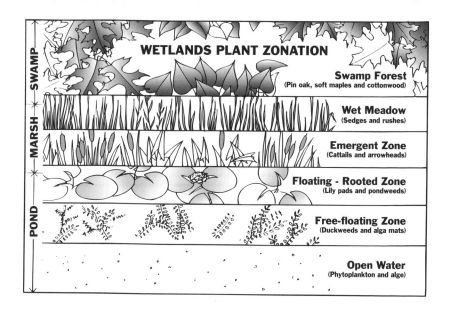

WETLANDS PLANT ZONATION

SWAMP

Swamp Forest
(Pin oak, soft maples and cottonwood)

MARSH

Wet Meadow
(Sedges and rushes)

Emergent Zone
(Cattails and arrowheads)

Floating - Rooted Zone
(Lily pads and pondweeds)

POND

Free-floating Zone
(Duckweeds and alga mats)

Open Water
(Phytoplankton and algae)

Marshes

Marsh vegetation develops in shallow, poorly-drained low-lying areas that can hold enough water most of the year to support soft-stemmed, rooted aquatic plants. Specialized plants grow in zones according to the depth of the water for which they are adapted. If the lowland area is a contained basin, the vegetation zones will move in from the edges to the center of open water, giving the marsh an appearance of shore-to-shore vegetation. When seasonal changes or local conditions raise or lower the water level, the character of the marsh will change as the plant patterns respond to the new level.

Wetland plant zonation

Marshes are very sensitive to environmental disruptions.

Emergent marshes, a particularly outstanding natural asset of Lake County, are found along the edges of the lake shore marshes and at abandoned channel ponds on the Chagrin and Grand Rivers. In their pristine state, these wetlands are home to sweet flag and several varieties of hard stem and soft stem bulrushes. The dominant species of an undisturbed marsh is the common bur reed. Currently, non-native hybrid cattail and phragmites, a tall plumed grass, have invaded and degraded many of Lake County's shoreline marshes, jeopardizing native marsh vegetation. The tall, winter-dried stalks of phragmites also pose springtime fire hazards to marshlands.

Phragmites invasion

Deep water pond at The Holden Arboretum

Aquatic Beds

A sand dam at a river mouth can back up water levels as much as eight feet above the current level of Lake Erie. Good examples occur at Arcola Creek and at the western end of Mentor Marsh near the Mentor Lagoon. The aquatic bed communities found in deep waters upstream from sand spits and within Lake Erie bays are becoming increasingly rare. American eel grass, yellow star-grass and a host of other distinctive, specialized vascular (veined, soft-stemmed) plants, as well as a number of pond weeds, once flourished in the clean, clear waters of river mouth bays and ponds prior to human activity in the area. Water marigold formerly occurred in Lake County but cannot be found today at any of its historical sites in Ohio.

Aquatic beds are important nursery, breeding and feeding areas for several species of fish that inhabit Lake Erie. Today, finding any of the deep water vascular plants that were collected 50 to 100 years ago at Mentor Marsh and the mouth of the Chagrin River is difficult. Only a few examples still prevail at the mouth of the Grand River. Occasionally, the vascular aquatic bed plants get entangled with fishing lines and are misidentified as algae or seaweed.

The turbid water conditions caused by pollutants in Lake Erie and the introduction of European water-milfoil probably contributed to the loss of native deep-water plants. Ironically, the filtration and clearing of lake waters by the recent onslaught of zebra mussels may set the stage for the return of some aquatic plants to the bay shores of Lake County. Man-made ponds, especially those at The Holden Arboretum and in the Lake Metroparks, have helped to preserve deep water plant species and habitats.

Upland Forests

Beech-Maple Forest

South of the lake plain and beyond the southernmost beach ridge, the land begins to rise for the next two to four miles until it reaches the edge of the Allegheny Plateau highlands. This rise, eroded bedrock blanketed by glacial deposits, is known as the Portage Escarpment. It is well drained, excluding the intermorainal lowlands, and was once covered by a beech-maple forest and a mixed mesophytic forest. The beech-maple association, dominated by slow-growing and long-lived (300-400 plus years) sugar maple and American beech, was once the most prolific forest community in northeastern Ohio. The beech-maple community was a continuous, vast, wilderness forest across much of the glaciated portions of Ohio and presented an impressive obstacle to 18th century settlers. When they first encountered the extent and density of these woods, early pioneers called it the "dismal forest".

Gradually, the beech-maple and the faster-growing mixed mesophytic forests were cleared to open the land for agriculture. Occasionally, a farmer would leave a stand of sugar maples as a sugar bush for collecting the sap that produces maple syrup. Bole Woods at

The Holden Arboretum and The A.B. Williams Memorial Woods at the Cleveland Metroparks North Chagrin Reservation are protected examples of a well-established beech-maple forest.

Bloodroot

Once a beech-maple forest has been cut down and the land used for agriculture, the beech-maple will not easily reestablish. Several stages of succession must occur first. Clear cutting for agriculture sets up conditions that favor domination of the land by other faster growing vegetation. As a result, the original extent of the beech-maple forest has declined significantly in recent years. Many of the fine stands still remaining were left intact only because they were sugar bushes associated with farms. Currently, throughout Lake County and northeastern Ohio, the last few unprotected stands are being decimated as they become prime sites for housing and commercial developments.

Trillium

Beech-Maple Understory

When left intact, a beech-maple forest is home to a broad range of wildflowers in its understory that are predominately spring bloomers. Among the spring bloomers is a well-defined group known as the spring ephemerals. They grow rapidly and achieve full bloom and maximum leaf expansion before the canopy tree leaves develop and shade the forest floor. Fruits ripen quickly, often within three weeks after flowering. The ephemerals have adapted to the light conditions imposed by the canopy.

Prominent wildflowers of this group include trout-lilies, Dutchman's breeches, squirrel-corn, toothworts, and spring beauty. Other familiar early spring bloomers abound but they differ from the ephemerals because the leaves are retained for a part of the summer, and usually the fruits ripen several weeks after flowering. Included in this group are wild geranium, two common trilliums (the white and the red), Jack-in-the-pulpit, wild ginger, bloodroot, mayapple, the hepaticas and various species of violets.

If the low-growing vegetation is severely grazed by domestic animals, the trees of the beech-maple forest may survive, but the understory will be damaged and limited in diversity for countless decades. In the past agricultural era, clear cutting of the forest was common and this practice produced a patchwork of beech-maple forest stands. Whenever a grazed forest stand is isolated by development, the reintroduction of wildflowers does not occur. As a result, many of the remaining beech-maple stands within Lake County and other areas of northeastern Ohio display an impoverished wildflower diversity.

Currently, large populations of white-tailed deer are now overgrazing and browsing all forest types in Lake County and are decimating the forest understory in much the same way, further preventing the return of a wider range of understory plant species, especially wildflowers.

River Corridor Plant and Tree Communities

The rivers and streams of Lake County have carved splendid valleys in their northward flow to Lake Erie. Sections of Lake County's two major rivers, the Chagrin and the Grand, have been designated as scenic by the state of Ohio.

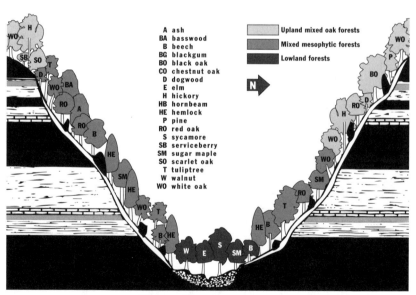

A	ash
BA	basswood
B	beech
BG	blackgum
BO	black oak
CO	chestnut oak
D	dogwood
E	elm
H	hickory
HB	hornbeam
HE	hemlock
P	pine
RO	red oak
S	sycamore
SB	serviceberry
SM	sugar maple
SO	scarlet oak
T	tuliptree
W	walnut
WO	white oak

Upland mixed oak forests

Mixed mesophytic forests

Lowland forests

River valley tree patterns

Vegetation varies significantly between the valley floor and the valley rim. The dominant plant communities change in response to drainage patterns and available light. However, mixed broadleaf forests are the most common community on sloping river-valley walls and on flood plain terraces.

Channel Pond Marshes

Rivers continually alter and recut their channels, especially during major flood events. Abandoned river channels often become wetland habitats, displaying the same diversity as a river-mouth wetland along Lake Erie shoreline. Channel pond marshes may contain aquatic beds, emergent marshes, swamp forests and shrub swamps.

Floodplain

The frequently flooded lowland adjacent to the river banks develops a distinct plant community in its thick, moist, silty soil that is similar to that of the lake plain wetlands. Shallow-rooted, fast-growing trees, such as sycamore, silver maple, and cottonwood, are the dominant species on river islands and flooded lowlands along streams.

Another dynamic natural community along the banks of the Chagrin and Grand rivers is the flood plain meadow. Open areas are created by ice-scouring that occurs with spring thaws and floods. Ice tends to keep woody vegetation growth at a minimum, and Emory's sedge usually establishes itself as the dominant builder of the lowland meadows. The sedge collects sediments and builds what appears to be lawn-like areas reaching out into the river. In the summer, the meadowlands support a wide assortment and

Big blue stem

abundance of colorful, summer-blooming wild flowers, including ox-eye, green-headed cone flower, joe pye weed, turk's cap lily and various prairie grasses such as big bluestem, Indian grass and prairie cord grass.

Butterflies are abundant. However, the recent invasion of phragmites and canary grass into these meadows is inhibiting other plant species. The changes pose a major challenge to conservation organizations.

Indian grass

Floodplain Terraces and Lower Valley Slopes
Mixed Mesophytic Forests

Adjacent to the major rivers are high terraces that once were the floodplains. Rich, mixed mesophytic forests with a diverse canopy of broadleafed trees occur on these terraces and on the lower valley slopes. The mesophytic forest displays diversity that is similar to the hummock-hollow mixed forest on the lake plain. Canopy dominants include tulip-tree, sugar maple, beech, black cherry, basswood, red maple, bitternut hickory, white ash, cucumber magnolia, red oak, white elm, red elm and shagbark hickory.

The tallest, most distinctive and most common mixed mesophytic canopy species is the tulip-tree. It is a marker for identifying this forest type. Tulip-tree is less common in a beech-maple or hemlock hardwood forest. Its towering, pyramidal shape is easily recognizable, especially in the fall. The brilliant, bright yellow autumn coloration of the abundant tulip-tree stands out dramatically among the reds and oranges of other species and gives valley slopes and terraces a golden glow.

Tulip-tree leaf

Jack-in-the-pulpit

The understory of a mixed mesophytic forest is home to a wide variety and spectacular abundance of spring wildflowers and ferns. Two of Lake County's rarest ferns, narrow-leaved glade fern and goldie's fern, are generally found only in this forest type. An explanation for the high diversity of wildflowers found within a mixed mesophytic forest as contrasted with the noticeable sparsity of wildflowers encountered in many beech-maple understories may be due in part to grazing. Historically, the floodplain terraces and lower valley slopes that support a mesophytic forest community were less accessible to grazing farm animals. Consequently, these understories were less disturbed and diversity tends to be higher.

Upper Valley Walls and Bluffs
Hemlock-Hardwood Forests

Moving upland from the valley floor, away from the terraces, the drainage is better and vegetation patterns change. Beech-maple and mixed mesophytic forests are frequently intermingled on upper valley wall slopes where soils are relatively deep. Often two distinctive forest types, the hemlock-hardwood and oak-chestnut, will occur on shallow soils as islands within the beech-maple and mixed forest, as well as on upper valley rims and highland sandstone and conglomerate outcroppings.

Hemlock

The hemlock-hardwood plant community and stands of white pine are generally found far to the north and northeast of Ohio. Northern hardwood forest species extend south into Lake County from Canada, western Pennsylvania and western New York. Hemlock signals the presence of other typical northern species, such as white pine and yellow birch. Prominent sites for the northern species are Lake County's snowbelt ravines. Usually, the trees favor the cool, north-facing valley walls of streams and rivers, and the shallow soils of conglomerate-capped uplands like Little Mountain and Chapin Forest.

White Pine Stands

White pine stands are scattered throughout the hemlock-hardwood forests. At one time, early botanists labeled white pines as possibly an isolated and restricted separate forest type that might be a relic from the Ice Age, but this is unlikely. The infrequency in distribution of the white pine is normal for this part of the world. White pine tends to persist in areas that have steep, exposed bluffs or sandstone platforms and are subject to periodic natural catastrophes caused by high winds and/or fire. A lightning strike, a tornado, or a line of Lake Erie squalls can decimate a hardwood stand leaving an opening for white pine to seed, thus setting the conditions for white pine occurrence. Little Mountain is a prime example.

White pine

Oak-Chestnut Association

Chestnut

South-facing valley walls tend primarily to support oak-chestnut forests usually dominated by white oak and black oak. This forest type is more common in the southern unglaciated portions of Ohio and the southern half of the Pennsylvania Appalachians, but it can occur also on sandy sections of the beach ridges and on bluff rims bordering the lakeshore. Unfortunately, chestnut has virtually disappeared from this forest due to the accidental introduction of chestnut blight several decades ago. Tulip-tree has replaced chestnut within many of the remnant oak-chestnut stands in Lake County.

In addition to white and black oak, most of Lake County's best quality oak-chestnut forests contain significant stands of chestnut oak. Just a few miles to the east in Ashtabula, chestnut oak becomes a very rare species.

Occasionally, trees of both the oak-chestnut forest and the northern hardwoods will occur on the same eroding rims along a river valley, especially in hogback areas like Indian Point and Hogback Ridge where tributary streams enter rivers. This combination is also found on sandstone uplands with shallow soils such as Little Mountain and Chapin Forest Reservation. At all these locations, both forest types are found in the canopy. In the open, oak-dominated sections of the canopy, the understory is home to several members of the rhododendron family, huckleberry, two types of low bush blueberry, and wildflower species, including spotted pipsissewa, Canada mayflower, smooth solomon's seal, smooth and downy false foxglove, and wild indigo.

Glacial Slumps

Valley wall slump at
Hach-Otis State Nature Preserve

One of the rarest plant communities in Lake County has developed along river valleys and is usually found on steep valley walls just below a rim that supports an oak-chestnut forest. A newly-named habitat, the glacial slump, is found in areas where a river is actively cutting away the base of a bank composed of mixed glacial tills or lacustrine deposits. Prime sites are the walls of the Chagrin and the Grand River valleys, which are composed of fine-textured clay and sand deposits. A slipping action is set in motion when water saturates the clay and sand, causing the deposits to "slump" away from the rest of the wall. Erosion appears to have scarred the landscape, but an interesting phenomenon occurs.

The table-like protrusions and steep slopes of a slump are very likely to support many plant species that are on Ohio's endangered and threatened lists. One of the rarest plants in Lake County, Cooper's milkvetch, was identified in a slump on the Grand River in Perry Township. Other interesting wildflower species, such as fringed gentian, grass-of-parnassus, and buffalo berry, can be found in a slump's open vents of blue clay. The most spectacular slump area in the county is in the Hach-Otis State Nature Preserve along the northern portion of the Chagrin River.

Ferns

A great diversity of native ferns can be found in Lake County natural areas. Most of the ferns are confined to woodlands and wetlands; but, one species, the bracken fern, forms large colonies in open barrens and old fields.

Bracken fern

Old Field Meadows

When the "dismal forest" covered most of Lake County, meadows were confined to the floodplains of the major rivers, abandoned beaver pond basins, eroding lake bluffs and possibly the lakeshore sandy beaches. With the clearing of the forest for agriculture, the range of this habitat was widened considerably. When farming declined in Lake County, hundreds of acres not under cultivation reverted to classic old field meadows filled with colorful summer-blooming wildflowers.

Queen Ann's lace, chicory and several annuals are the first to appear in a field the year after it is abandoned; in subsequent years, natural fields are dominated by perennials.

In the late spring and early summer, Lake County old fields are dominated by naturalized grasses and wildflowers that originated in Europe. Five European grasses, meadow fescue, red-top bent-grass,

Old field display of Queen Ann's lace

orchard grass, timothy, and Kentucky bluegrass grow quickly through May and flower in early summer. Tall buttercup, ox-eye daisy, several hawkweeds, clovers and bird's-foot trefoil produce rich color and pattern through June. As the season progresses, native plants become more obvious and by late summer native asters and goldenrods cover the meadows. These tall flowers are important sources of nectar for honey-producing insects.

Under normal conditions old fields are invaded by aggressive scrub vegetation and the wildflowers and grasses are replaced by trees and shrubs; but annual mowing can prevent this succession and perpetuate a field meadow.

Showy wildflowers that grace old meadows include Canada lily, common penstemon, mountain mints and black-eyed Susan. Bird species, like the American robin, which are rare in the forest, have become more common due to the increase of open field areas. Other bird and insect species associated with the prairies further west have also moved in. Lake County, as well as the rest of Ohio, is now home to a wide variety and

Ox-eye daisy

abundance of butterflies and moths. An old field meadow may seem somewhat ordinary, but it is a habitat of tremendous diversity that deserves close attention.

Roadside Plants

Salt-tolerant plants, halophytes, are relative newcomers to Lake County. Recently, several plant species, usually found in western salt flats and Atlantic coast salt marshes, have moved into Lake County and have become established along highways, salt storage areas, and salt mine sites. Seaside goldenrod, western sea-blite and several salt-tolerant grasses can be found along the guard-rails of four-lane highways throughout Lake County. Seaside goldenrod is one of the most showy species. Researchers at The Cleveland Museum of Natural History have also found beetles and flies native to salt water areas associated with the Lake County salt-tolerant plants.

Wildlife and Habitats

Just as the geology and climate of Lake County determine its vegetation, so does the vegetation determine the communities of wildlife that can inhabit the region. From Lake Erie's beaches and wetlands to the upland hardwood forests, Lake County is home to a diverse array of wildlife. Some species are closely tied to specific habitats while others range widely across the county.

Lake County has experienced a number of habitat transformations over the past two centuries as county lands were transformed from primeval habitats to agricultural, industrial and residential applications. Because human activity can alter the landscape and effect dramatic changes in natural systems, the vitality of many wildlife populations depends either on the adaptability of the species to human activity or on careful preservation of their special habitat requirements.

Historic image of
the primeval forest

Historic Forests

The remaining stands of mature forest protected by The Holden Arboretum and Lake Metroparks at Bole Woods and Chapin Forest offer a view of the Lake County landscape as it appeared to the first Europeans settlers.

In the past two centuries nearly all of the forest has been harvested at least once to clear the land for agriculture and settlement. Most of the present day woodlands are secondary growth forests.

The formerly extensive primal forest teemed with a variety of animals. Woodland bison, elk, white-tailed deer, lynx, bobcat, cougar, gray wolf, black bear, marten, fisher, river otter, porcupine, snowshoe hare and beaver were found in Ohio and most likely in Lake County. Today, nearly all have vanished from the county. Hunting pressures and the destruction of their forest habitat led to the disappearance of these species in northeastern Ohio. The bobcat still remains on the Ohio Division of Wildlife Endangered Species list but it, too, has become extinct in Lake County. A few large mammals are currently experiencing a comeback. White-tailed deer and river otter have been reintroduced, and recently, beaver has recolonized Ohio from neighboring states.

Passenger pigeon

One of the most dramatic features of the historic forests of Ohio was the extraordinary numbers of passenger pigeons. These large doves nested in the beech-maple forests and consumed beechnuts and other seeds. They clustered in huge communal associations and were a favorite food-market bird in the 18th and 19th centuries. Demand was so great that by 1914 hunting pressures, coupled with the wholesale harvest of its forest habitat to agriculture, led to the extinction of the passenger pigeon. Wild turkey vanished from Ohio for similar reasons, but the species has been reintroduced in the forests of northeast Ohio by the Ohio Division of Wildlife.

Today's Forests

Lake County is a crossroads of forest associations. Each forest type provides a variety of wildlife habitats and niches. Bird and mammal species that coexist within the forests of Lake County are each adapted in style to a unique location and opportunity in the woodlands. Some bird species are confined to a specific forest type. For example, dark-eyed juncos, solitary vireos, winter wrens, black-throated green, magnolia and Canada warblers nest only in the hemlock ravines along the southern flank of Lake County. Other bird and mammal species freely range across several habitats. A good example is the raccoon which requires some woodland habitat for a tree cavity den, but also forages along streams and rivers, in fields and in residential yards.

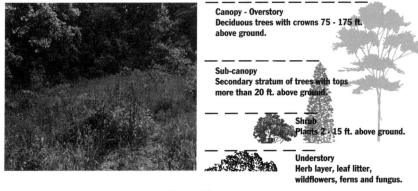

Canopy - Overstory
Deciduous trees with crowns 75 - 175 ft. above ground.

Sub-canopy
Secondary stratum of trees with tops more than 20 ft. above ground.

Shrub
Plants 2 - 15 ft. above ground.

Understory
Herb layer, leaf litter, wildflowers, ferns and fungus.

Forest layers

The structure of the forest provides a diversity of niches. The canopy, sub-canopy, shrub layer and floor are all utilized by wildlife. Some species are confined to a single stratum like the cerulean warblers, which only use the canopy. Other species, squirrels for example, forage at all levels in the forest.

A forest, like any habitat, provides feeding opportunities for wildlife that feeds upon plants and plant products, other animals or both. The forest also hosts organisms that feed on the dead remains of other organisms and play the vital role of decomposer. The forest forms a complex system of nutrient and energy cycling that is critical to the survival of all members of the forest community. The plants and animals are dependent upon each other and upon their physical environment.

Forest Birds

Birds expend energy rapidly for body heat and flight. They have extremely fast metabolic rates that require high-caloric diets of seeds, fruit or animal protein.

Many breeding birds of the forest eat invertebrates and can be sorted by their diet, foraging style, and location. A close look at the Lake County bird species populations in specific areas of the forest, from "top to bottom," will reveal very specific feeding habits.

Insect-Eaters

Cerulean warblers, scarlet tanagers, rose-breasted grosbeaks and great-crested flycatchers glean insects from the canopy of the forest. Eastern wood-peewees, Acadian flycatchers, yellow-throated vireos, and red-eyed vireos, probably the most common breeding birds in mature stands of a beech-maple forest, work the sub-canopy zone to find large insects. American redstarts can be observed diving for insects in "flycatcher" style between the shrub layer and the subcanopy. Hooded warblers tend to forage from the ground to the shrub layer, while ovenbirds feed in the leaf litter and among the herbaceous vegetation.

Red-eyed vireo

Two members of the thrush family, the American robin and the wood thrush, forage on the ground for worms and other large soil invertebrates. The Louisiana water thrush forages along streams that run through mature woodlands. Thrushes are noted for the distinctive and complex chord-like tones of their songs. The master of the group is the wood thrush whose flute-like calls at dusk embody the wildness of a rich woods just as the common loon's yodel embodies the wildness of a northern lake.

Birds that depend entirely on an insect diet are migratory during the cold winter months when insects are inactive.They must travel to warmer climates to find feeding opportunities. Most of the warblers, tanagers and flycatchers winter in the tropical, moist forests of South and Central America. The future health of these species is closely tied to protection of the great rain forests of the tropics.

Standing dead timber provides feeding opportunities for a variety of woodpeckers: the pileated, red-bellied, hairy, downy and the northern flicker. These species excavate insect runways and bark beetle galleries, (passageways in the logs,) and use their long, barbed tongues to stab and extract the insects. The flicker spends much of its time foraging directly on the ground, often in meadows or open spaces with widely-spaced trees. The graduated size of the various species of woodpeckers is associated with the species' food resources, each to the appropriately-sized insects. The tree cavities excavated and used by woodpeckers for nesting sites are later occupied by other species. All of these woodpeckers, except the northern flicker, remain in Lake County through the winter. Most of their insect prey is available in the bark and rotting wood of decaying trees. Cavities used for nesting in the spring offer protection against extremes in weather and become roosting sites in winter.

Pileated woodpecker

In A. O. Beamer's *A Natural History of Lake County, Ohio* published in 1940, both the red-bellied and the pileated woodpeckers were considered rare. Today, the red-bellied is common and the pileated is widely distributed and seen throughout the mature forests and even in Lake County backyards. The change is due largely to a reversal in land use. Vast tracts of land, formerly cultivated in the 19th century, have gradually regenerated to forests, thus increasing the habitat potential for these species of woodpecker.

Red-headed woodpeckers are found in association with scattered, open oak forests, river bank habitats, woodland edges and swamp forests. They catch insects on the wing as well as explore bark beetle galleries for food. Though primarily migratory, some red-headed woodpeckers may winter over, frequenting well-stocked bird feeders or subsisting in large part on acorns, beechnuts and unharvested grain.

Seed-eaters

Representing the seed-eaters in the forest are the black-capped chickadee, the tufted titmouse, the northern cardinal and the blue jay. These species may be opportunistic insect eaters in the summer months, but seeds and nuts are the basis

Eastern phoebe

of their diets in the winter. The blue jay feeds on acorns and beechnuts but is also an opportunistic predator, eating insects and occasionally stealing eggs or nestlings of other species.

Tufted titmouse

Birds of Prey

Birds of prey in the forest include the red-shouldered hawk, broad-winged hawk, Cooper's hawk, eastern screech owl and barred owl. The red-shouldered hawks feed on small mammals, reptiles and amphibians during the day. Barred owls feed at night consuming large numbers of short-tailed shrews that are common in leaf litter and the upper soil zone.

Barred owls, screech owls and broad-winged hawks also consume large numbers of insects in addition to small forest

Barred owl

mammals. The Cooper's hawk specializes in catching small to medium-sized songbirds. Great-horned owls and red-tailed hawks typically forage in more open habitats such as fields, but both require a mature forest or woodlot for roosting and reproduction, preferring at least a square mile of range.

Forest Insects

Zebra swallowtail butterfly

Most of the "moving parts" of forests are insects. They provide the essential services of pollination and decomposition as well as food for most birds, mammals, fish, amphibians and reptiles. In a Lake County beech-maple forest, over 500 species of moths and butterflies occur, each with caterpillars that specialize on a select group of plants. For example, the fat, green caterpillars of the luna moth are found high in the canopy of beech, wild cherry and hickory trees; the bark-like caterpillars of the sweetheart underwing moth are well-camouflaged on cottonwoods; hidden under the dead leaves on the forest floor are the small Idia moths, and the caterpillars of the zebra swallowtail butterfly are found only on pawpaw.

Many forest insects are silent and hidden, except in summer, when some of them become very noisy and obvious. Annually, the dog-day cicadas can be heard buzzing loudly. However, the periodical cicadas reveal themselves with deafening song only every 17 years.

Forest Mammals

Bats

Bats are well distributed through Lake County. Species include the big brown bat, little brown myotis, the silver-haired bat, hoary bat, the red bat and several others. These flying mammals are adapted for catching flying insects on the wing by using their superb powers of echo-location. Moths and other night-flying insects form the bulk of their diet. Bats are usually crepuscular, active at dawn and dusk, and most often seen at twilight. Their activity patterns are influenced by the habits of the insects upon which they feed.

Because insects are dormant in cold weather, the food supply for bats is unavailable in winter. Some, such as red and hoary bats, migrate while others hibernate. During hibernation, the bat's metabolism slows down causing a significant drop in body temperature and conservation of energy resources through the long winter months. Bats hibernate in caves, hollow trees, barns, attics or other secluded areas. They are often reviled as carriers of rabies or feared as a threat to human health. In fact, bats are no more likely to carry rabies than other wildlife species, and they avoid contact with people. Their seemingly erratic flight paths, which occasionally come close to humans, is a function of their pursuit of insects with erratic flight paths. Bats play a significant role in controlling over-abundant insect populations, particularly mosquitos.

Squirrels

The forests of Lake County host a variety of rodent species, the most conspicuous being the members of the squirrel family. The large, hoary squirrel common to many backyards is the fox squirrel. These squirrels bury acorns in the lawn, build leafy ball-shaped nests in treetops, and raid the local birdfeeder. The smaller red squirrel is associated with conifer groves and specializes in eating pine seeds and cones. Recently, a black form of the gray squirrel was released in The Holden Arboretum area and has expanded its range in the southern part of Lake County.

Gray squirrel

Flying squirrels are widely distributed throughout the forested areas of Lake County. They spend daylight hours denned-up in old woodpecker holes, coming out only at night to forage for seeds and nuts. Not true flyers, these large-eyed squirrels are equipped with skin flaps between their fore legs and rear legs and a flat, rudder-like tail that together enable them to glide from one tree trunk to another.

Chipmunks, small members of the ground squirrel family, animate the forest floor with their rapid foraging movements and their repetitive chirp call that resounds through the forest in spring and summer.

Shrews and Mice

Common in the leaf litter of the forest are short-tailed shrews whose frenetic movements under the leaves are sometimes heard but seldom seen. These small, insect-eating mammals have exceedingly high energy requirements to maintain their fast-paced metabolic rates. Shrews forage continually throughout the day and night, searching for soil invertebrates

Short-tailed shrew

and mice. The toxic saliva of the short-tailed shrew can paralyze prey even larger than the shrew itself, such as a mouse. Several other species of shrews also occur in Lake County, but none is armed with toxic saliva and so are confined to feeding on small prey.

Rodents frequenting forested areas include several species of mice such as white-footed mice, deer mice and woodland jumping mice. Their great numbers provide the quantity of prey necessary to sustain many of the large predators such as hawks, owls, foxes and snakes.

Raccoon

Many species of medium-sized mammals thrive in woodland, agricultural and residential habitats. Raccoons, with their familiar black masks and banded tails, enjoy a wide distribution within Lake County. Traditionally considered woodland omnivores with a fondness for foraging in wetlands, they now frequent suburban chimneys, and glean garbage from trash cans. Their distinctive footprints with delicate long toes and wide reach are a common sight in the mud or sand along any watershed. Raccoons eat crayfish, freshwater clams, fish, tadpoles and frogs, and eggs and nestlings from a variety of birds and reptiles. Fruit, seeds, nuts and vegetable matter also form part of their diet.

Opossum

North America's only living marsupial, the opossum, is a common inhabitant of Lake County and has a wide distribution throughout most of Ohio. The opossum moved into northern Ohio during the clearing of forests for cultivation in the 19th century. Being omnivorous like raccoons, opossums frequent agricultural areas where they forage for waste grain, rodents, insects and carrion.

Skunk

The striped skunk ranges widely across the county, with large numbers found in suburban locales. This portly member of the weasel family uses its stout forelegs and claws to turn over leaf litter and forage through the top layers of humus in search of moles, shrews, mice, small snakes, amphibians and invertebrates. A skunk 's omnivorous habits make it well-adapted for life in the suburban yard where it will overturn sod to consume soil invertebrates such as worms and beetle larvae, and rummage in trash bins for food.

Skunks are noted for an acrid-smelling, oily spray that they can release from anal scent glands and aim in the direction of any potential enemy within a range of 5 to 10 feet. As the liquid strikes, it is absorbed by the hair and skin of the victim, and the odor persists for days or even weeks. This form of chemical warfare is unique to skunks among North American mammals.

Foxes

Three non-domestic members of the dog family are found in Lake County: the red fox, the gray fox and the coyote. The red fox inhabits the forest edge and open fields. Only the gray fox inhabits woodlands and is unique among these canids for its ability to climb trees. Foxes

are opportunistic hunters of small mammals, birds, reptiles and amphibians and use their highly developed sense of smell to locate prey. Long thought of as bloodthirsty killers of domestic fowl, foxes are now better known as having prodigious appetites for rodents. Foxes usually den in burrows in the ground.

Red fox

Deer

Today, only one large mammal occurs in Lake County woodlands, the white-tailed deer. Although deer were extirpated in Ohio by the turn of the 20th century, the Ohio Division of Wildlife reintroduced them in 1930. This event, along with the increasing immigration of deer from neighboring states, has restored the deer population in Ohio. The current population, estimated at 300,000, is actually

White-tailed deer

greater than it was in the days prior to pioneer settlement of the area. Deer require cover provided by forests, but they forage in edges near woods where shrubby vegetation is within reach. Due to the fragmentation of Ohio's woodlands and an increase in bordering shrubs, deer now have a broader range of feeding opportunities available than ever before. The current success of deer can be attributed both to easy access to food and to the extirpation of their natural predators.

Forest Reptiles and Amphibians

Garter snake

Reptiles

The reptiles of Lake County's forests include snakes, turtles and one lizard. An interesting woodland snake is the black rat snake, Ohio's largest snake, that grows to eight feet in length. This sleek black snake with white mottling on its belly is an accomplished climber and can ascend vertical tree trunks, using the rough bark for scaling upward. Like all snakes, the black rat snake is predatory and stalks other reptiles, amphibians, small mammals and birds. At present, none of the snakes found in Lake County is venomous, although the Massassagua rattlesnake inhabits swamps and wet meadows in nearby Ashtabula and Trumbull counties.

One of the few lizards found in Ohio, the five-lined skink, has been recorded in Lake County. It is typically found in woodlands under leaf litter, rotted logs, near rock or brush piles or in other moist conditions. The skink is characterized by a bold blue tail that attracts the attention of potential enemies. The attacker usually grabs the tail which detaches from the skink's body. The lizard escapes leaving the attacker with a mouthful of squirming tail. Over time the skink will regenerate a modest new tail.

The eastern box turtle is the only turtle in Lake County that utilizes a terrestrial woodland habitat. It can be found shuffling through the forest leaf litter in search of soil invertebrates, fruits and vegetable matter. Its name refers to the hinged plastron, a shield, that closes over the head, legs and tail of the turtle giving it protection from forest predators such as the skunk, raccoon or opossum.

All Ohio reptiles survive the cold winter months by retreating into abandoned burrows of other animals or into deep soil pockets beneath the leaves. Cold-blooded animals can survive the otherwise deadly conditions of winter by getting below frost line, the zone of ground about three feet below the surface that does not freeze during the winter. Aquatic reptiles retreat into the mud at the bottom of a pond, swamp or marsh.

Amphibians

Lake County supports a diversity of amphibians - frogs, toads and salamanders. Several species of salamander inhabit rotting logs or rocks or between rock ledges. Vernal pools, temporary pools that form after the snow melts but dry up before the end of

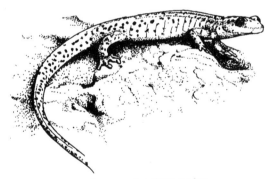

northern red salamander

summer, are important breeding sites for amphibians. Mole salamanders, such as the spotted salamander and the Jefferson salamander, emerge from their subterranean haunts with the first rains in March and migrate to ancestral breeding ponds where they participate in a reproductive rendezvous. Eggs, deposited in the ponds, hatch into larvae that develop over the course of the summer, transforming into adults before the ponds dry-up in late summer. Because these ponds are temporary, they contain no fish, so the egg masses are subjected to little predation.

Some species of amphibians migrate to ponds and lakes to complete their reproductive mission. American toads congregate in large numbers in the shallows of Lake County ponds and rivers in late spring. The males 'sing' long musical trills that attract females. Wood frogs, spring peepers, and gray treefrogs also join in this springtime ritual that attracts females of their own species, fulfilling the amphibian destiny of belonging to two worlds - water and land.

The red eft, a terrestrial form of the red-spotted newt, has a conspicuous orange body with red spots. This coloration is in great contrast to the earth tones of its habitat. The warning coloration signals potential predators that the eft is toxic. When a predator attacks this salamander, a secretion is released from its skin that irritates the mucous membranes of the predator's digestive tract. The eft is disgorged. Though the eft might not survive the event, the predator will shun efts as a food source. The red eft matures into the aquatic red-spotted newt that inhabits ponds and swamps in the county.

Open Field Habitats

Large fields are a common sight today in Lake County, but until the 19th century, they were rare. The only natural breaks in the forest canopy were blowdowns, storm damage, burned areas and successional stages following the abandonment of beaver ponds. Occasionally, Native Americans would clear a few acres of flood plain or river terrace for crop cultivation. As land was converted from forest to pasture or hayfield by the settlers, the process provided extensive opportunities for open country birds to expand their range in Lake County. In the history of the birdlife of the county, the most dramatic changes have been made by open area species that rapidly colonized agricultural areas. By the turn of the 20th century, the landscape of Lake County was largely cleared and open. Species of wildlife that were adapted for such habitats flourished. Many forest birds, however, did not fare as well.

Open Field Birds

The eastern meadowlark, bobolink, grasshopper sparrow, vesper sparrow, field sparrow, Henslow's sparrow, red-winged blackbird, upland sandpiper, loggerhead shrike, barn owl, indigo bunting, red-tailed hawk, American kestrel, and turkey vulture established large breeding populations. Most of these species had been present in the few open clearings in the forest. They quickly adapted to pastures and cultivated fields as opportunities arose. Many soon became the most common birds in the county as more acres were converted for agriculture.

New trends in land use have led to a reduction of the grassland and hayfield habitats of the early 1900s, which in turn has hindered some grassland species from maintaining their populations.

Ring-necked pheasant, introduced to Ohio in 1896, reached peak numbers in the state by 1933. The bird has not tolerated the loss of fence row habitat and the recent transition of grasslands to forest. Populations are now in decline.

The decreasing number of barn owls seems related to the reduction of grassland and the concurrent decline in meadow voles, the owls' principal prey. Declines in upland sandpipers and loggerhead shrikes are also attributed to this phenomenon. Meadowlarks, bobolinks, grasshopper

Ring-necked pheasant

sparrows, and savannah sparrows are experiencing a drop in numbers with the disappearance of pasture lands.

Eastern bluebirds forage in open grasslands but require nest cavities in trees for successful reproduction. The introduction of the European starling poses a significant threat to the bluebirds because starlings fight aggressively for similar nest holes. The Holden Arboretum and Lake Metroparks are managing a program to rebuild bluebird populations by placing starling-proof nesting boxes in strategic locations throughout Lake County.

Open Field Mammals

Many mammals fared well with the opening of the Ohio landscape. Grass eating species exploited the feeding opportunities on farms, particularly pastures, alfalfa and hay fields, and crop lands. These habitats were made even more attractive by the presence of underbrush, fencerows, and overgrown borders between fields and along woodland margins. Eastern cottontail rabbits, meadow voles and groundhogs are species that thrive in open fields.

Rabbit

Cottontail rabbits are found in a variety of open field, old field and forest edge. They were not common in the great forests of antiquity in Lake County, but they quickly expanded into the farmlands. Cottontail rabbits are now a very

common animal in the county and throughout Ohio flourishing in a variety of habitats, including the residential yard. Rabbits feed on most types of vegetable matter although their greatest numbers are usually associated with areas of fertile soils. Apparently the quality of forage is important to their survival. Rabbits are an important prey species for red foxes, great-horned owls and red-tailed hawks.

Groundhog

Groundhogs are the largest members of the squirrel family and are widely distributed in Lake County. They are frequently seen along the roadside in agricultural areas where they assume an erect posture on their hind quarters to scan for predators. Like other rodents, they possess two pairs of continually growing incisor teeth that allow them to eat a wide variety of plant materials. Groundhogs excavate extensive burrow systems that can range nearly a 1/4 acre underground. Their bedding chambers are above the access runways. The low spots in the runways allow for proper drainage of the burrow. A burrow network will have one or two main entrances, with adjacent large mounds of fresh dirt, and secret or emergency entrances that are well camouflaged and sometimes pose a fracture hazard to any large animal that walks over them. Groundhogs are true hibernators, retiring to warm and secure burrows in November and emerging in late February or early March. When in hibernation, their body temperature drops dramatically, metabolic rate lowers, and energy stores are conserved through the winter. Amusing myths and legends associated with the length of winter surround the groundhog's hibernating schedule.

Old Field/Shrub Habitats

Old fields, fields that are not in current cultivation and have been allowed to develop weedy and shrubby conditions, are home to several mammal species and display a great diversity of birds, particularly where field and forest meet.

Old Field Mammals

Red Fox

Red fox exploit old fields and underbrush woodland edges. Although dog-like in form, this predator is often catlike in behavior as it stalks small rodent prey and leaps into the air, pouncing down and pinning a mouse under its forepaws. Fox are attracted to habitats that favor the cottontail rabbit, a major prey species. Red fox often utilize denning burrows located just inside a woodland edge. The fox has scent glands near its anus that produce a skunk-like musk odor which is used as a scent marker to define its territory.

The origin of Ohio's present red fox population is uncertain. Fox were undoubtedly in the area at the time of early settlement, but also may have been introduced by colonials from the eastern states in the mid-1700s to enhance the population for sport hunting.

Coyote

Coyotes are also members of the dog family and are associated with open field in Ohio. Their range over the continent has been extended eastward dramatically in the 20th century pushing from the western prairies into the agricultural land of Ohio. Although not common in Lake County, coyotes are present.

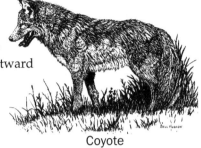

Coyote

The diet of this medium-sized hunter is comprised mainly of woodchuck, rabbit and mice. The coyote is not well suited for hunting large mammals such as an adult deer, but may take an occasional fawn. Though capable of killing sheep or other domestic livestock, coyotes are probably less damaging to stock than wild dogs.

Old Field Birds

Gray catbirds, brown thrashers, indigo buntings, blue-winged and yellow warblers, and song sparrows are usually present in large numbers in thickets and woodland edges. Field sparrows, white-eyed vireos and yellow-breasted chats favor this shrub-stage successional habitat.

Openings in the overgrowth provide places for a springtime ritual performed by the American woodcock. At dusk on a clear March or April evening, the male woodcock leaves his clearing and takes to the air. As he spirals upward the outer feathers of his wings create a soft twittering sound barely

American woodcock

perceptible to the listener. When he reaches the apogee of his flight, he swoops earthward calling a series of liquid descending notes until he returns to his clearing. Any female woodcock in the area is attracted by his acrobatics and approaches his clearing where they mate. The female will nest on the ground near the margins of the old field where it meets the forest's edge.

Ruffed grouse are found in second growth forests and in dense thickets, generally near water. In the past, the bird's preference for young, second growth forest and forest edge limited its range to fire-scar and blowdown areas and old beaver meadows. Ruffed grouse populations exploded across the state in the mid-1800s when harvesting of the primeval forest maximized the shrubby and second growth conditions that grouse prefer.

Old Field Reptiles

Eastern garter snakes are the most common snake found in Lake County. This handsomely striped snake rarely exceeds three feet in length. The eastern garter snake feeds on mice, toads, frogs, insects and invertebrates that are found in open field habitats. Milk snakes, blue racers and black racers also hunt the open and semi-open field areas.

Old Field Insects

In old field/successional habitats many European weeds and non-native agricultural plants have become established. Some of the insects are exotic as well: Chinese and European mantids; Japanese beetles; one- third of the species of leafhoppers; and German and European hornets.

Several moth and butterfly species use specific old field plants for food while in their caterpillar phase. Native milkweeds nurture a truly American insect, the monarch butterfly. As a caterpillar it eats only milkweed. Plantain is used by wooly bear caterpillars to mature into Isabella moths, and violets host the caterpillar of the showy, fritillary butterfly. The

Monarch caterpillar on milkweed

regal fritillary is becoming very rare because the particular species of violet it needs in its caterpillar phase, the bird's foot violet, only grows in wetlands. When wetlands are drained for development, the habitat for the violet and the butterfly are destroyed.

61

Monarch butterfly

In August, fields become very noisy as tree crickets begin to sing. Along the edge of some old fields, out of harm's way from tractors and just far enough out to catch the sun, ants build their mounds. Herds of aphids and buffalo treehoppers can be found on nearby golden rods and viburnums.

"Backyard" Wildlife

As Lake County becomes increasingly urbanized, suburbanized, industrialized and homogenized, less and less wild and open space remains for wildlife. While that has negative impacts on those species that require natural habitats, some species are adapting well to suburban habitats.

Butterflies and Moths

Butterflies and moths will visit backyards to gather nectar. They can be enticed by planting flowers that produce abundant nectar, such as butterfly bush, sedums, phlox and milkweed. Red admiral butterflies will approach from nearby nettles while tiger swallowtails will appear from cherry and tulip trees. Plantings of parsley or dill may nurture black swallowtail butterfly caterpillars within a garden. Use of many pesticides will decimate butterfly populations.

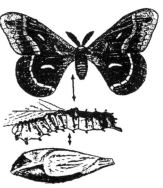
Cecropia moth

Birds

Song sparrows, northern cardinals, blue jays, American robins, and others species that are well-suited to backyards and small farmsteads have increased in population. Bird species that take advantage of feeding stations, such as the black-capped chickadee, the tufted titmouse, the red-breasted and white-breasted nuthatch, the hairy woodpecker and downy woodpecker, are common in backyards. The northern cardinal was not observed in Ohio at the time of early settlement. It has extended its range into northeastern Ohio over the past two hundred years and is now the official state bird.

Backyard birds

62

The 20th century saw the introduction of house sparrows, European starlings and house finches. Rock pigeons, escaping from farms and breeders, became well established. Common grackles, brown-headed cowbirds, red-winged blackbirds, and northern crows, thriving on produce from the farm fields, all increased in numbers as open conditions were made accessible.

The cowbird is a species of significance because it is a brood parasite; the female lays her eggs in the nests of other species of birds. The hatchling cowbird is usually larger and more vigorous than its nest mates and often kills them by pecking them, pushing the eggs from the nest or outcompeting them for food from the foster parents. Many bird species in open habitats have mechanisms that deal with the cowbird. For example, yellow warblers will build a new layer of nest material over the foreign egg and their eggs as well and produce a new clutch of eggs. Woodland species do not have the means to fend off the cowbird, and they are often its victims.

Mammals

Several mammal species have been successful in suburban habitats, and their populations are on the rise. Raccoons and skunks often forage in garbage cans and compost heaps. Rabbits are commonly seen in gardens plots, and white-tailed deer are becoming frequent backyard visitors as woodland acreage is converted into housing tracts.

Shoreline Habitats

Lake Erie exerts a strong influence on the condition and types of habitats that occur in the northern half of Lake County, especially along the shoreline. Resident shoreline plant communities and wildlife species are sensitive to lake conditons, water levels and wave action.

The geographic position of Lake Erie is particularly critical for migrating birds.

Migrating Birds

In the spring, Lake Erie serves as a barrier to the northward movement of raptors (birds of prey) which are reluctant to cross open water. They fly along the lakeshore and cross into Canada near Buffalo or continue around the western end of Lake Erie to head north. Hawk migration peaks in mid-to-late April.

Northern pintail ducks

Most species of song birds are able to cross Lake Erie. Often they are seen gathering along the lakeshore awaiting suitable weather and flight conditions for their crossing.

A diversity of waterfowl graces the waters of Lake County. Several migrating species annually stage and feed in the marshes, estuaries and protected waters of Lake County's shoreline. Tundra swans move through the area in March and November, sometimes in flocks numbering in the hundreds. Occasionally, they will settle on large inland lakes in smaller numbers. Shallow-water feeding ducks, dabbling or puddle ducks, can be found throughout the wetlands between March and May and again from September to November. Diving, or bay, ducks and mergansers can be seen on Lake Erie during winter months, clustered at the warm-water discharge areas of the electric generating plants in Eastlake and Perry. Thousands of common goldeneye, lesser and greater scaup, redhead, canvasback and common and redbreasted mergansers gather along the Lake Erie shoreline in winter.

Bald eagle

Occasionally a bald eagle is sighted. The national bird was probably a common nesting species in Ohio a few hundred years ago. As recently as the 1950s, bald eagles nested in neighboring Ashtabula County. Lake shore development, coupled with environmental contamination, has greatly reduced the number of eagles present in Ohio.

The Mentor Marsh State Nature Preserve, Mentor Headlands State Park and Nature Preserve, and Fairport Harbor Lakefront Park are widely recognized as some of Ohio's premier birding areas. It is not uncommon for more than 100 species to be recorded by birders on a single May morning. Documented sightings at Mentor Marsh reveal that at least two hundred species of birds, both resident and migratory, use this important Lake County wetland as a staging area or breeding habitat.

The sandy beach at Mentor Headlands State Park provides a remnant of a once widespread habitat. In migration, sanderlings, whimbrel and other beach shorebirds may be sighted. Huge flocks of blue jays can be seen streaming out of cottonwood trees, uncharacteristically silent as they head north in April and May.

Migrating Insect Populations

In the fall thousands of monarch butterflies make their way across Lake Erie from Ontario, Canada, sometimes forming clusters along the southern shoreline as they rest overnight. The monarchs are migrating to Mexico, to mountain refuges just northwest of Mexico City. There, they will winter over on the Oyamel firs. In March, they head northeast; the first females arrive in Lake County in mid-to-late May.

Resident Shoreline and Wetland Birds

Shoreline Birds

The lakefront attracts a variety of gull species. Ring-billed, herring and Bonaparte's gulls congregate by the thousands at the generating plants and the Lake County solid waste site in Perry. Their numbers peak in December and January. Other gull species tend to congregate with this large resident gull population. For example, greater black-backed gulls, little gulls and glaucous gulls have been recorded as lakefront visitors in recent Christmas Bird Counts completed by birding organizations.

Herring gull

Wetland Birds

All the shoreline wetlands and interior wetlands of Lake County host a variety of birds. Red-winged blackbirds, northern yellowthroats, marsh wrens, Virginia rails, soras, green-backed herons and least bitterns are birds of the cattail marshes and estuaries in the county. Swamp sparrows and yellow warblers are denizens of the willows and dogwood thickets along the margins of wetlands. Canada geese, wood ducks, and mallards nest in swamp and inland ponds or near the larger marshes. The wood duck flirted with near extirpation a century ago due to the loss of large trees offering cavity nest sites. With the return of forests and the widespread use of nest boxes, predator-proof and placed in optimum sites, the wood duck is now commonly found nesting in suitable habitats throughout Lake County.

Wood duck

Purple martins forage intensely along the water's surface in pursuit of winged insects, as do tree swallows and rough-winged swallows. These species prefer nest cavities in dead trees or birdhouses erected near water.

Before 1950, Canada geese did not nest in Ohio. Their presence was usually noted in the massive spring and fall migrations as they staged in protected waters. With the introduction and widespread use of aerators to maintain open water in winter, the conservation of ponds and feeding programs that conditioned geese to stay in certain areas, a sizeable breeding population took hold throughout Lake County. Today, Canada geese inhabit nearly every lake, pond, marsh, swamp, river, and roadside ditch.

Canada goose

Shoreline and Wetland Mammals

Cattail marshes are occupied by muskrat, furred rodents with a sinuous, black, nearly hairless tail. Muskrats feed on marsh vegetation and build lodges from cattails and other marsh materials.The lodges appear as low mounds in the marsh. Muskrats are the preferred prey of mink, a relative of the weasel and skunk. Though not numerous in Lake County, mink, prized for its pelt, is usually found in pristine and undisturbed marshes and wetlands.

The star-nosed mole is a common wet meadow resident. Mole activity is easily identified by the long, raised ridges of soil that mark the forging trails of this nearly blind mammal. The snout of the star-nosed mole is festooned with 22 pink, fleshy, finger-like tentacles protruding from the edge of the nose in a star-like pattern. The tentacles serve to heighten tactile awareness as the mole feels its way through the swamp. The star-nosed mole is equipped with powerful pectoral muscles and broad, flipper-like forepaws with strong claws to dig tunnels. Shallow tunnels are dug to locate food such as worms, beetle larvae and other soil invertebrates. Deeper tunnels provide forage in winter and a safe place to rear young. Some burrows open directly into water; these moles can swim and are thought to be capable of catching aquatic prey. Unlike other moles, the star-nosed mole spends considerable time on the surface or in very shallow tunnels, making it vulnerable to hawks, owls, skunks and other predators.

Shoreline and Wetland Insects

Wetlands host myriad insect species, especially shoreflies. Several species of dragonflies and damselflies hover and sprint over marshes. Water striders ride atop the water's surface on graceful legs designed not to break the water's surface tension.

Water strider

Behind the dunes at Mentor Headlands State Park is the fragile habitat of the hirticollis tiger beetle. The species once was common on sandy shores of the Great Lakes, but destruction of its shoreline environmment has made it rare. The hirticollis tiger beetle larva digs a burrow in the damp sand where it waits in ambush for passing prey, using its flattened head to close the burrow opening.

Clouds of large chironomids, nonbiting midges, occur on shoreline bushes. These are the adult forms of small larvae that grow and feed underwater in Lake Erie. In the dunes are the diggerwasps which catch other insects or spiders to place in their burrows as food for their larvae.

River and Stream Habitats

Lake County has two primary watersheds, the Chagrin River with its East Branch and the Grand River with Big Creek and Paine Creek, two of its largest tributaries. Lake County is fortunate to have watersheds that are among the cleanest in Ohio. Sections of the Chagrin River have the distinction of being designated as Scenic by the Ohio Division of Natural Areas and Preserves. A portion of the Grand River in Lake County is designated as both Wild and Scenic.

Watershed Birds

The rivers and their heavily wooded valleys provide habitats for a diverse array of bird species. Great blue herons, emanating from the Munson Township rookery in Geauga County, forage in shallow waters in search of fish, frogs, invertebrates and other aquatic organisms. Belted kingfishers nest in burrows in eroding banks; their rattling cry can be

Great blue heron

heard as they fly up and down the river valley seeking fish. Bank swallows inhabit similar banks, flying above the rivers feeding on insects with hawk-like maneuvers. Spotted sandpipers forage in the mud flats and along the shoreline for invertebrates.

Watershed Insects

There are 77 species of dragonflies and damselflies in the Grand River watershed. Different species live in slow water and in fast water: the small yellow-green clubtail and the black-shouldered spinyleg live where the river widens and runs slowly, whereas, the yellow green clubtail and the yellow-headed clubtail live where the river narrows and flows faster through a gorge. The adults rest on the floodplain sedges and "hawk" for their insect prey while the immature nymphs live under the water.

Ten-spot dragonfly

Watershed Mammals

Raccoon

The river valleys are prime foraging habitat for raccoons that come to the water's edge seeking amphibians, invertebrates and fish. Their distinctive footprints are commonly seen in mud or sand along the water.

Beaver

The beaver has re-established in Lake County over the past 30 years and is now well distributed in smaller streams. Famous for its engineering feats, beaver construct dams, create ponds and erect large domed lodges. Chisel work on trees and shrubs along the banks of a stream is visible evidence of the presence of beaver in the area.

Beaver is Ohio's largest rodent. As is characteristic of all rodents, the beaver's evergrowing incisor teeth are covered with hard enamel on the front side and softer dentine on the interior side. As the beaver gnaws, the back wears faster than the front and maintains a sharp, chisel edge to the incisors. This self-sharpening system is essential in downing small trees for sustenance and construction materials. Aspens, willows and birch are favored by beaver as food sources.

The beaver's wood-harvesting and dam-building activities can greatly influence a river bank woodland landscape.

Otter

The river otter disappeared from Ohio due to overharvesting of the mammal, and watershed pollution which caused the extinction of several fish species critical to the otter's diet. In recent years the

River otter

Ohio Division of Wildlife has initiated a restoration program along the upper reaches of the Grand River in Trumbull County. If the releases prove successful, and breeding populations thrive, the otter, which roams extensively, will soon occur throughout Lake County.

Aquatic Habitats

Fish populations in Lake County have changed substantially over the past 200 years in response to overharvesting and changing aquatic ecology brought on by human activity. With the clearing of the forests, soil erosion became a major factor affecting water quality. Increased siltation led to a reduction in water clarity, which in turn had a profound effect on plant and animal species intolerant of dirty water. The introduction of carp into Lake County rivers at the turn of the 20th century contributed to the problem. Carp are notorious for churning up mud and silt deposits in a marsh or estuary. Whitefish, sturgeon, and lake trout were among the early casualties of overharvest, poor water quality, new competitors, and parasites. The opening of the Welland Canal in 1825 brought an invasion of the sea lamprey into the waters of the Great Lakes and inadvertently introduced marine parasites to native fish species.

Lake Erie

By the 1960s, Lake Erie was in distress as a fresh water habitat. Industrial pollution and the decay of huge blooms of algae led to oxygen depletion in the lake. Several species of fish succumbed as did vast numbers of mayfly larvae. Lake Erie was once famous for its burrowing mayflies which would mature and come ashore in June and July in such numbers that tree branches would break from their weight. In 1969, oxygen conditions were so severe that Lake Erie was in jeopardy of becoming a dead lake.

Game Fish

Since that time, pollution control measures and clean-up efforts have greatly improved water quality, and Lake Erie is recovering its ability to sustain diverse life forms. Many species of game fish are enjoying an increase in numbers. The presence of

Walleye

walleye and yellow perch have contributed to a renewed interest in sport fishing.

Exotic species, such as coho salmon and steelhead, have been introduced to attract the interest of the fishing community.

Some exotic species in Lake Erie continue to be a concern. The recent introduction of the zebra mussel in ballast water discharged into Lake St. Clair from a European cargo ship is an example. In just a few years the small mollusk established itself throughout Lake Erie. The far reaching consequences of huge zebra mussel populations are still unassessed. The question that remains is whether predators in the lake can rise to this new feeding opportunity or whether the zebra mussel will replace the remaining native freshwater clam populations in Lake Erie and its tributaries.

Steelhead

Inland Lakes and Ponds

Fish

Inland lakes support populations of white and black crappie, smallmouth bass, northern pike, bluegill and sunfish. The best examples of traditional farm pond habitats are at The Holden Arboretum. At breeding time, sunfish and bluegills can be observed guarding their nests in the shallows of most ponds.

Bluegill

Frogs - Toads - Turtles

Tadpoles of toads, green frogs, bullfrogs and pickerel frogs are easily spotted along a pond or lake edge. Midland painted turtles basking in the sun are conspicuous on emergent logs, particularly when air temperature is dramatically higher than water temperature.

The quiet, deep recesses of ponds and lakes are suitable habitat for the snapping turtle. Looking like a creature from the age of dinosaurs, this mighty predator leaves the water only when the female lays her eggs. She might travel dozens of miles in search of the right place to deposit her leathery-shelled 'legacy'. The snapping turtle is Ohio's largest turtle and has been known to exceed 30 pounds in weight. In its aquatic surroundings, the snapping turtle will scavenge as well as take live prey. In spite of its formidable appearance, it is not a threat to humans.

Snapping turtle

Insects

Shallow lakes and ponds are rich in aquatic insects: water boatman, backswimmers, whirligig beetles, dragonflies, and damselflies, toe-biters and water scorpions, mayflies and caddisflies. Some, the dragonflies and caddisflies, for example, live in the water only as nymphs. Immature caddisflies construct little houses, which they drag over the bottom of the pond. Others live in the water even as adults. The water boatmen, backswimmers, and whirligig beetles can swim underwater even as adults and can pop up through the surface to fly away.

Left: Stonefly
Right: Mayfly

Native American Inhabitants

After the Ice Age and before the arrival of European settlers, the Lake County region was occupied by Native American populations.

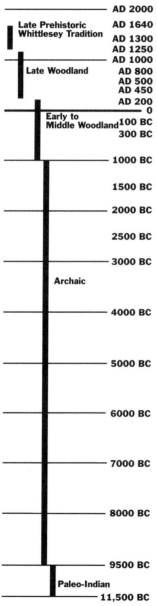

Chronology of Lake County Prehistoric Indians

- AD 2000
- AD 1640 — Late Prehistoric Whittlesey Tradition
- AD 1300
- AD 1250
- AD 1000
- AD 800 — Late Woodland
- AD 500
- AD 450
- AD 200
- 0
- 100 BC — Early to Middle Woodland
- 300 BC
- 1000 BC
- 1500 BC
- 2000 BC
- 2500 BC
- 3000 BC
- Archaic
- 4000 BC
- 5000 BC
- 6000 BC
- 7000 BC
- 8000 BC
- 9500 BC
- Paleo-Indian
- 11,500 BC

Prehistoric Paleo-Indians (11,500 - 9500 B.C.)

The prehistory of Lake County began after the retreat of glacial ice about 14,500 years ago. Herds of caribou migrated from the north along the cedar swamps fringing the shore of the Erie basin. Inland, moose and mastodons browsed on the hemlock and birch that grew around cold lakes and bogs. The first scattered families of humans to inhabit northeastern Ohio, Paleo-Indians, are known from isolated finds of distinctive chipped-stone "fluted" spear points. These "Clovis" points show only minor changes from 11,500 to 9500 B.C. In southern Lake County, reports of Clovis points come from what were probably small campsites on gravel kames (ridges) overlooking post-glacial kettle lakes.

Clovis point

Archaic Period (9500 - 1000 B.C.)

The noteworthy cultural adaptations of early populations during the Early Archaic Period (9500 to 8000 B.C.) reflect the changes in environmental conditions that occurred in northeastern Ohio at that time and which continue today. The scope of the cultural changes was revealed recently at a site dated to 7900 B.C. along the Aurora Branch of the Chagrin River. Gone were the moose and mastodon. Deer, bear and waterfowl were hunted instead by native groups.

72

During the warmer Middle (6500 to 3500 B.C.) and Late (3500 to 1000 B.C.) Archaic Periods, the small family groups of hunters and gatherers grew larger as they improved their economy. They developed nets to fish in Lake Erie and skillfully used the food and medicinal plants that grew in the forests of the Lake County region. Like their neighbors throughout the Lower Great Lakes, the Archaic inhabitants of the county discovered how to grind and polish granite and basalt into axes, chisels, mortars and pestles, and they learned to make a spear-throwing tool out of wood and stone or bone.

This Indian petroglyph, found in Lake County, can be seen at the Lake Erie Indian Museum

Early to Middle Woodland Period (1000 B.C. - 450 A.D.)

The introduction of pottery and the intensive collection of local plants are characteristic of the Woodland Period. Family bands gradually became clans of near-sedentary gardeners, who collected vast quantities of nuts and grew squash, sunflowers and a variety of seeds to supplement their hunting and fishing.

The Early Woodland (1000 to 100 B.C.,) "Adena" and the Middle Woodland (100 B.C. to 450 A.D.) "Hopewell" people of southern Ohio built large complex earthworks and mounds, and they developed extensive trade routes. Although few such spectacular mounds exist in Lake County, Cleveland Museum of Natural History archaeologists have discovered several small fishing camps along Lake Erie's shore that yielded types of early Woodland pottery dated to 950 B.C. Spear points of the same period have been excavated from several small hunting camp sites along Big Creek.

Other finds have provided insights to this period. At a site between Perry and Madison, archaeologists found a bark keg filled with Adena or Hopewell spear points that had been ceremonially sunk in a bog. Along the lower Grand River bluffs, a Hopewell mound opened in the 1800s was found to contained elaborate spear points of Arkansas stone. A few years ago, museum excavations on the opposite river terrace revealed a fire pit in a small campsite where several pots filled with nuts, acorns, and wild leeks had broken and burned sometime between 180 A.D. and 230 A.D.

Late Woodland Period (500 - 1250 A.D.)

During the early part of the Late Woodland Period, Native Americans in the Lake County region adopted the bow and arrow for hunting deer, elk and raccoons. They also began living in larger groups and started subsistence farming with crops of corn, squash and tobacco. One warm season site near the junction of the Chagrin River and the East Branch was occupied by as many as five families. Along portions of the Grand River bluffs, cold season sites were built, occupied, and then abandoned.

In addition to domestic sites, early Late Woodland peoples built walled ritual precincts on some steep ridges. Granite was chipped and used for knives and arrow points. Pieces of slate and shale were made into tools for heavy woodworking , smoking pipes and various ornaments. Bone and shell were also used in the fabrication of tools, beads and musical instruments.

Women made the family pottery and distinctive techniques were passed from generation to generation within a given group. Studies of similarities and differences in the way the pottery was made reveal a great deal about the relationships of interacting families. Research shows that the Lake County groups were closest to other family groups that lived along the lake shore from western Cuyahoga County to

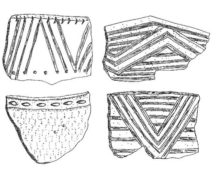

Pottery chards with pattern variations

northeastern Ashtabula County. They were not as socially close to the inland groups that were geographically near in Geauga, Portage and Trumbull Counties.

Late Prehistoric Period/The Whittlesey Tradition (1250 - 1640 A.D.)

The Late Prehistoric Period culture of Lake County is called the Whittlesey Tradition. Along the Grand River, Whittlesey summer farming sites grew larger and were occupied for longer periods of the year. Rock shelters were used during winter hunts, and several large spring and fall fishing camps existed at the mouth of the Chagrin and Grand Rivers and along Indian and Ashtabula Creeks.

In northeastern Ohio, the final Whittlesey phases run from A.D. 1450 to about A.D. 1650. Most late Whittlesey people lived year-round in large villages of 10 to 15 multi-family houses covered with mats or bark. Crops of maize and beans were cultivated on sheltered pockets of the fertile flood plain to support the families. The villages were protected by palisaded ditches and embankments or were built on high isolated plateaus overlooking the flood plain, 3 to 8 miles up river on the Cuyahoga , Grand, and Chagrin Rivers.

Several Whittlesey sites in Lake County have been thoroughly excavated. Although people of the Whittlesey culture occupied the area until 1650 A.D., none of the materials found suggests that this native group had even indirect contact with Europeans.

Settlers Alter the Landscape

Pre-settlement Conditions

When Europeans first entered northeast Ohio in the 1700s, they found the land just as the Native Americans had long known it. Lake Erie, its beaches and dunes bounded the north backed by a forest of towering trees whose canopy dimmed the sunlight. Hemlock and white pine darkened the east and north-facing slopes of the Grand and Chagrin River valleys. Game abounded—bear, lynx, cougar, elk, wolf, beaver, fox, and deer. Waterfowl and shore birds were plentiful as were wild turkey, grouse and quail. Passenger pigeons were so numerous that their weight sometimes broke the branches on which they roosted.

First Settlers

French explorers and trappers entered the region before 1700 and by 1750 a trading post had been established at the mouth of the Chagrin River. Once the word began to spread about the seemingly limitless supply of natural resources in Ohio, enterprising New Englanders were prompted to look westward after the Revolutionary War. The Connecticut Land Company was formed in 1795 to survey and sell land in the northeastern section of Ohio known as the Western Reserve. It wasn't long before the network of Native American hunting and trading trails became well-worn wagon traces and later became the foundations of the east-west roads which are still in use today. By 1797, a route was proposed from the Pennsylvania line to the Cuyahoga River. General Simon Perkins was hired to oversee the project. He proceeded to cut a 33-foot-wide swath through the forest by "girdling" the big trees to hasten the process. This method made clearing easier because it disrupted the flow of nutrients to the tree, causing it to die and dry out. (The site of his surveying camp is marked today

A "corduroy" road - logs laid side by side to traverse a wetland

on Girdled Road in Concord Township). By the end of 1797, the first settlers' cabins were built near Mentor Marsh.

Transformed Wilderness

Trumbull Mill on the Grand River

In the early decades of the 19th century, Lake County's vast resources stimulated economic growth in northeastern Ohio. Abundant supplies of timber and sandstone for building materials, game for food and fur, bog iron for manufacturing, and plentiful water brought and kept settlers. Fertile land was cleared and numerous farming communities were established. Sawmills, grist and woolen mills, brickyards and factories sprang up. The ancient beach ridges that once were the shores of glacial lakes became major roadways. Trees were felled and the logs laid side by side forming "corduroy" roads through marshlands. Swamps were drained and rivers bridged.

Because of their small numbers, the Native Americans lived in relative balance with their environment; the settlers' impact on the area was far greater. Ohio was quickly being transformed from a wilderness into a cleared territory that supported a mechanized and industrialized society created by the newcomers from New England and Europe.

Early Naturalists Mid - 19th Century

The "Arkites" - early northeast Ohio naturalist group

The opening of the Ohio territory attracted the best naturalists of the day. Prominent 19th century botanists began documenting Ohio's native plant species. Their early work would establish the baseline for future generations to recognize that natural resources are not limitless. In 1810, Thomas Nuttall, a renowned British botanist, walked the beach ridge road from Erie, Pennsylvania west through Painesville to Huron. He was among the first to include some of the plants along the Lake Erie shoreline in his *Genera of North American Plants* (1818). Botanist Constantine Rafinesque also followed the lake trail between Fairport and Sandusky, recording Ohio plant species and noting them in his *New Flora of North America* (1836-38).

Interest in what was below ground was also gaining momentum. Land speculators frequently lied to prospective buyers about the mineral deposits "just waiting to be dug." Even geologists of the day did not have reliable information.

77

In the 1830s, the Ohio General Assembly voted to commission a geological survey of the state. William W. Mather was appointed to head the first (1837-38) of three surveys conducted during the 19th century. The surveys were important, not only for determining the economic prospects of Ohio's mineral deposits, but as the first overview documentation of the state's flora and fauna.

Northeastern Ohio physician and naturalist, Dr. Jared Potter Kirtland (1793 -1877), made significant contributions to the 1838 survey. He came from Connecticut in 1830 to settle in the Western Reserve. While living in Lake County and teaching in the medical department of Willoughby University of Lake Erie, he actively pursued study of the natural history of Ohio and built a reputation as a foremost American naturalist. He corresponded frequently with other important Ohio naturalists to exchange theories and compare findings. Dr. Kirtland was instrumental in founding The Cleveland Academy of Natural Sciences in 1845 to formally establish the exchange of information. The Academy, later renamed The Kirtland Society of Natural History, evolved into The Cleveland Museum of Natural History.

Documentation of the natural history of Ohio was becoming more precise. The 1873 Ohio Geological Survey included the first description of Lake County's bedrock sequences recorded by M.C. Read and accompanied by detailed maps. Dr. Henry Curtiss Beardslee of Painesville assembled the *Second Catalog of Plants of Ohio* (1874); his son H.C. Beardslee, Jr. was one of America's leading mycologists who identified a number of mushroom species. Adrian A. Doolittle of Painesville (1876-1943), a skilled field ornithologist and bird-bander, recorded Lake County native bird populations for the U.S. Biological Survey.

Conservation Movement - Early 20th Century

By the first half of the twentieth century, Ohio natural scientists began to note the rarity of some species and the apparent extinction of others throughout the state. Bear, elk and lynx vanished from northeastern Ohio. Fish populations diminished. The last passenger pigeon died in the Cincinnati zoo in 1914. Concern was mounting and a conservation movement was gaining momentum across the country influenced by the writings of Henry Thoreau and John Burroughs.

Early logging operations alter the Lake County landscape

"May Hike" - 1933

Area naturalists tried to heighten citizen awareness and appreciation of wildlife and resources. In 1916, a handful of Lake County residents got together in Willoughby and subscribed to the books of John Burroughs. The informal meetings of this group evolved into the Burroughs Nature Club with life-long bird expert Frank N. Shankland as its first president. It continues to this day as a respected forum promoting the need for conservation in northeastern Ohio. The enthusiasm and camaraderie of the Lake County naturalists impressed many distinguished Ohio natural scientists who made a point of joining the annual Burroughs Nature Club "May Hike" bird survey, which the group initiated in 1921.

When Charles M. Shipman came to Willoughby from New York in 1917, he joined wholeheartedly in the growing cause of conservation, especially to help maintain Lake County assets. He was an early member of the Burroughs Nature Club and set to work on the conservation of Mentor Marsh, Little Mountain and Gildersleeve (Chapin Forest), Starve Island, Headlands Beach, Fern Lake and the Hach-Otis woodland. His stirring lectures, exquisitely illustrated with glass lantern slides, undoubtedly influenced many people. A keen naturalist and photographer, he also championed the protection of birds of prey.

C.M. Shipman was instrumental in pushing for the purchase of the Blackbrook area by the state of Ohio for state park usage. In 1938, the Blackbrook Nature Club was formed in Painesville and became an active chapter of the National Audubon Society in 1958. Blackbrook members are dedicated to a very active program of conservation and education. Involved private citizens support the work of local, state and national conservation agencies and organizations that are trying to maintain environmental balances in an age of rapid changes. The conservation of Lake County's natural heritage could not be achieved without the dedicated efforts of such committed individuals.

Although the early naturalists might be dismayed at the changes in Lake County, they would rejoice in knowing that a number of their favorite haunts are in good hands. Many of Lake County's pristine natural areas are carefully conserved and used actively in educational programs which instill an appreciation of Lake County's rich natural heritage in new generations.

Conservation Challenges to Lake County

Lake County communities have experienced rapid growth in recent years. As development continues, there will be substantial changes in natural resources that can affect wildlife habitats and populations. The changes will also have an impact upon plant communities, soil and water quality, and on resources with geological, historical and archaeological significance as well. Several issues arise which must be considered. The effect of these changes on the quality of life in Lake County will depend upon carefully planned growth and conservation efforts.

Wildlife

The direct relationship between human activity and native wildlife activity is a concern. As habitats are altered and certain wildlife species adapt to suburban areas in greater numbers, more human-wildlife interactions will occur. Many of these will be negative. A visit to the Wildlife Rehabilitation Center at Penitentiary Glen Reservation provides evidence of the conflicts. The crippling effects of car strikes, window strikes, acute toxicity, entanglement with fences, and orphaned wildlife are readily apparent.

As forests become more fragmented, many bird species that depend upon interior forest habitat will be at risk in the coming years. A single road cut through a forest can drastically alter its habitat potential. Every forest has an edge around its perimeter where open country predators, brood parasites and nest cavity competitors can gain access to the forest habitat. Interior forest species are safe only deep within the forest. If the forest is dissected by a road or partially logged, the change increases the amount of edge habitat relative to the interior. Aggressive edge species, such as the cowbird, will thrive, while deep wood species, such as thrushes, forest warblers, and tanagers, will decline because they are poorly equipped to deal with cowbird parasitism.

The current decimation of tropical rain forests, as well as the decline of temperate forest acreage in Ohio, has ramifications for Lake County birds that migrate to, and winter over in Central and South America. If those distant habitats are destroyed, migratory species that use both habitats and breed in Ohio will disappear. Currently, declines in populations of ovenbirds, wood thrushes and red-eyed vireos, for example, are thought to be a result of fragmentation of these forests.

When wooded lands are developed, the remaining forests become islands in a sea of suburbia. The potential for free interchange among wildlife populations is dramatically reduced and can have negative genetic consequences for the wildlife species that are forced to inbreed within the confines of these islands.

Conservation and maintenance of large tracts of forest with corridors of habitat to link them is the only solution to this severe biological problem. Conservation efforts directed toward the wooded Chagrin and Grand River valleys are of key importance to the habitats and wildlife of Lake County.

Diversity is critical to all plant and animal life cycles. The diversity of wildlife in Lake County is a heritage to be safeguarded. The wild creatures that dwell here not only enrich our lives, but serve as indicators of the quality of the environment we all share. It is important to be deeply aware and concerned about maintaining viable and genetically healthy wildlife populations in the area. This goal requires strong commitment to conserving the variety of scenic and biologically distinct habitats still remaining in Lake County.

Waterways and Wetlands

Streams, ponds, wetlands and lakes play an important role in the water cycle that is crucial to all living things. Precipitation percolates into the ground water, runs off into rivers and streams, is transported by plants back into the atmosphere or is held in wetlands, ponds and lakes until it evaporates. Water quality may be jeopardized anywhere within this cycle. Siltation and pollution from commercial and residential development can threaten water reserves. Conservation and protection of waterways is essential to maintain water quality in Lake County.

Streamways and wetlands are not only valuable scenic attributes but are essential as rich and productive habitats. Historically, swamps, swales, bogs, river bottoms, and marshes were regarded as worthless, unproductive lands fit for little other than mosquitoes. That view has been discarded because in recent years the vital role of these biological powerhouses has been documented. Wetlands minimize flooding and act as pollutant filters. Forested stream corridors keep water temperatures cool and help control erosion. The lake shore provides not only unlimited recreational potential for people but critical habitat for migratory and resident animals.

Over the past 200 years many of Lake County's prime wetlands have been drained or compromised. Most of the lakefront has been developed, and with increasing urban expansion, the forested streams of Lake County are experiencing residential development pressure. Careful planning is essential to protect the remaining waterways and shoreline from over development.

Native Plant Communities

Due to its many unique features, a great diversity of plant life exists in Lake County; however, very little of Lake County's native plant communities have been left intact due to developments initiated by the pioneers and which continues today. Protected natural areas contain many of the best examples of native plants. Even these areas are under threat of alteration by the invasion of European and Asian plant species and by the foraging of certain animal populations.

Intact native plant communities not only provide information about Lake County's past, but they may also provide future resources for medicine and food. It is important that these plants be properly managed and protected while their role is being documented and analyzed. Currently, efforts are underway to catalog and inventory the botanical resources of Lake County to protect unique species from eradication.

Land Use

Dramatic changes have occurred in the Lake County landscape. Initially, the early settlers encountered a heavily forested region. For most of the 19th century, Lake County was extensively cleared and farmed. In the past 50 years, agriculture in the county has declined and abandoned farmland is returning to forest.

Areas that are still dedicated to agriculture, located primarily in the sandy soils of the lake plain or in the vineyard regions along the Grand River, have proven to be a unique resource to Lake County. The quantity and quality of the horticultural and vineyard products from these lands generate a cash value that is the third highest of all agricultural sales in the state of Ohio.

Even these agricultural resources, as well as other resources, are under threat again as new options for land use arise. Residential development is now occurring at such rate in Lake County that it is becoming increasingly difficult for landowners to maintain their properties as open space. Increased property values almost assure that land will ultimately be consumed by residential land use.

Land use issues must be resolved and balanced in order to protect the very qualities that make Lake County an appealing place to live and work.

Environmental Issues

Environmental contamination of the region remains a threat. Pesticides, herbicides and industrial and home use chemicals continue to be released into the environment. Many of the compounds have severe consequences as they infiltrate the water cycle and the food chain. The chemicals become concentrated in the bodies of wildlife faster and in greater amounts than they accumulate in water or air. Toxins affect the health of an animal and may adversely affect its reproductive abilities as well. Many of these pollutants may compromise the health of humans as well.

Conclusion

Past and present resource and land use in Lake County has a long-lasting impact. As the county developed, the enormity of the changes to the environment and landscape prompted the early naturalists and conservationists to take action to protect the resources of the region. That tradition must continue. The future of Lake County's natural heritage depends upon the stewardship of today's citizens. Every Lake County resident and visitor can take an active role in conservation by supporting the organizations and agencies charged with safeguarding Lake County's natural resources.

Conservation Resources

How to go beyond this book

Numerous public and private groups, organizations and local, state and federal agencies are involved in natural resource conservation in Lake County. They offer Lake County residents and visitors a variety of volunteer and educational opportunities to learn more about natural history and conservation efforts. Everyone can become an active participant in conserving the natural heritage of Lake County.

State Agencies

State of Ohio Department of Natural Resources

Fountain Square
Columbus, Ohio 43224
614-265-6540

Division of Natural Areas and Preserves

614-265-6540

Division of Parks and Recreation

614-265-6561

Division of Wildlife

614-265-6300

Ohio Environmental Protection Agency

1800 Water Mark Drive
P.O. Box 1049
Columbus, Ohio 43266
614-644-3020

Local Agencies

Lake Metroparks

11211 Spear Road
Concord Township, Ohio 44077
216-639-7275

Lake County Cooperative Extension Service

99 East Erie Street
Painesville, Ohio 44077
216-357-2582

Lake County Soil and Water Conservation District,

125 East Erie Street
Painesville, Ohio 44077
216-357-2730

Cleveland Metroparks

North Chagrin Reservation
3037 SOM Center Road
Willoughby, Ohio 44094
216-473-3370

Organizations

The Holden Arboretum

9500 Sperry Road
Mentor, Ohio 44060
216-946-4400

The Cleveland Museum of Natural History

1 Wade Oval Drive—University Circle
Cleveland, Ohio 44106
216-231-4600

Burroughs Nature Club

4588 River Street
Willoughby, Ohio 44094

Blackbrook Audubon Society

7573 Dahlia
Mentor, Ohio 44060

The Indian Museum of Lake County

on the campus of Lake Erie College
(Managed by the Lake County Chapter of
The Archaeological Society of Ohio)
391 West Washington Street
Painesville, Ohio 44077
216-352-1911

Lake Metroparks, The Cleveland Museum of Natural History and
The Holden Arboretum have collaborated to produce this edition of *A
Natural History of Lake County, Ohio.* They each have a history of land
and resource conservation and have acquired significant properties in
Lake County which are managed for the purpose of conservation in
perpetuity.

Lake Metroparks

In 1917, legislation was adopted in Ohio to permit the creation of county park districts. While often associated with the county government, park districts are actually political subdivisions of the State of Ohio. Each park district has a board of three commissioners appointed by the probate court.

State law provides Ohio park districts with the power to pass levies, adopt rules, hire staff and "acquire lands for conservation within or outside the county of the park district's origin for conversion into forest reserves, and for the conservation of the natural resources of the state, including streams, lakes, submerged lands and swamplands, and to those ends may create parks..." The general philosophy of most park districts in Ohio regarding park land development has been to conserve 80% and to develop 20% for public recreation areas.

In 1958, Lake County Park District was established. The history of land ownership by the Lake Metroparks began in 1959 with the donation of land at the confluence of Big Creek and the Grand River that is now the Helen Hazen Wyman Park. Since that time, through other donations, grants, and purchases, the Lake Metroparks land base has expanded dramatically. Most of the park lands are located along the Grand River and two of its major tributaries, Big Creek and Paine Creek.

Lake Metroparks has also secured properties on the lake shore, the lake plains, the Chagrin River, and the Sharon Conglomerate outcroppings on the Portage Escarpment. The Park District will continue to acquire additional lands to conserve Lake County's natural heritage.

The vast majority of park lands are reservations or natural areas with little, or no, development. The park system provides hiking trails, picnic grounds, interpretive educational areas and special use recreational facilities where appropriate.

Within the park lands located throughout the county, a tremendous diversity of plant and animal communities can be found. A biological inventory of these communities provides important information that is helpful to Lake Metroparks in protecting fragile areas, promoting unique natural features, and placing facilities.

In addition to providing public access to the best examples of every major habitat in Lake County, Lake Metroparks offers a broad range of educational and recreational programs that encourage an appreciation of Lake County's natural history.

The Holden Arboretum

The Holden Arboretum is a major Lake County institution and one of this country's most outstanding arboreta. It was established in 1931 on 100 acres of land in Kirtland Township to promote the study and conservation of plants for ornamental purposes and scientific research. Today, The Holden Arboretum covers over 3100 acres in Lake and Geauga counties, and has documented living collections of 3800 different plant species. They include the crabapple, hedge, maple, conifer, and nut tree collections, and the rhododendron, wildflower, and display gardens.

In addition to undertaking horticultural research for scientific, educational and aesthetic purposes, a significant part of The Holden Arboretum' s mission is to develop and maintain documented collections of woody plants and other botanical specimens appropriate to the climatic zone of northeastern Ohio, and to study, manage and conserve the natural environment of the arboretum's lands.

The Holden Arboretum is the largest arboretum in the country and is unique in that 75% of its 3100 acres is under natural cover. Holden reserves include some of northeastern Ohio's most pristine natural areas. From Pierson Creek Valley to the summit of Little Mountain there is an elevation change of over 500 feet that provides Holden with a rolling topography and dramatic vistas. The Holden Arboretum's natural areas, including the Stebbins Gulch reserve and Bole Woods, represent a broad spectrum of Lake County's plant communities and geologic history. Meadows, ponds, wetlands, mature hardwood forests and hemlock-lined ravines are accessible. Some of the preserve areas are unique and support rare and unusual plants, especially on Little Mountain. The Arboretum staff offers guided hikes through these fragile areas.

The Holden Arboretum is unique in offering a blend of horticultural collections and varied natural areas to explore and enjoy. With 20 miles of trails, it provides an opportunity to rediscover Lake County's natural landscape as it may have appeared to the early settlers of the Western Reserve.

The Arboretum offers a schedule of events featuring a wide selection of classes, walks and hikes that highlight both horticultural and natural history subjects.

The Cleveland Museum of Natural History

The Cleveland Museum of Natural History is nationally recognized for its collections, exhibits, educational programs and publications. Since its inception, the Museum has been dedicated to research in the natural sciences and to heightening appreciation of the natural environment.

Early in its history, the trustees and staff realized the need to provide services beyond the confines of the museum to encourage public awareness of northeastern Ohio's natural heritage.

In the 1930s, The Cleveland Museum of Natural History was instrumental in establishing the Cleveland area's first metropolitan park nature trails and the first trailside nature interpretive centers. For several years the Museum managed The Holden Arboretum, The Cleveland Aquarium and The Cleveland Zoo. Many of these early projects are now autonomous and the respective organizations maintain a strong working relationship with the Museum.

Currently, among its many new projects, the Museum is involved in a Natural Areas Program to acquire and conserve the best remaining examples of Ohio's natural heritage for biological surveys, scientific studies and stewardship projects. For this reason, the Museum is a major landholder in Lake County, owning or leasing over 700 acres.

The Museum works in joint effort with the State of Ohio Department of Natural Resources to identify significant natural resources to be designated as scenic and wild areas, protected as wetlands, or dedicated as reserves.

Nine northern Ohio reserves are managed by the Museum including Mentor Marsh State Reserve and four areas within the Grand River drainage basin. Amphibian, bird, mammal, insect and plant populations are being inventoried and studied by Museum staff in cooperation with Lake Metroparks, The Holden Arboretum, and The Ohio Department of Natural Resources. The Museum also conducts ongoing research of sites within Lake County that have geological or archeological significance.

The Cleveland Museum of Natural History is an invaluable resource that provides opportunities to learn about all aspects of natural history, especially the natural history of northeastern Ohio. In addition to extensive permanent and temporary gallery exhibits, the Museum offers classes, lectures, field trips, live animal programs and planetarium programs.

Additional Reading
Geology

Banks, P., and R. Feldmann, editors, *Guide to the Geology of Northeastern Ohio*. {Cleveland}: Northern Ohio Geological Society, 1970.

Carter, C., *Living with the Lake Erie Shore*. Durham: Duke University Press, 1987.

Glacial Geology

White, G., *Glacial Geology of Lake County Ohio*. Columbus: Ohio Division of Geological Survey, Report of Investigations No. 17, 1980.

Chorlton, W., *Ice Ages*. Alexandria: Time-Life Books, 1983.

Pielou, E., *After the Ice Age*. Chicago: The University of Chicago Press, 1991.

Botany

Ohio Wildflowers: Let Them Live in Your Eye Not Die in Your Hand. Columbus: Ohio Department of Natural Resources, 1990.

Ohio's Trees. Columbus: Ohio Department of Natural Resources, 1990.

Andreas, B., *Vascular Flora of the Glaciated Allegheny Plateau Region of Ohio*. Columbus: Ohio State University, Ohio Biological Survey, 1989.

Braun, E., *The Woody Plants of Ohio*. Columbus: Ohio State University Press, 1961.

Newcomb, L., *Newcomb's Wildflower Guide*. Boston: Little, Brown and Co., 1977

Birds

Peterjohn, B., *The Birds of Ohio*. Bloomington: Indiana University Press, 1989.

Peterjohn, B., and D. Rice, *The Ohio Breeding Bird Atlas*. Ohio Department of Natural Resources, 1991

Rosche, L., editor, *Birds of the Cleveland Region, second edition,* The Cleveland Museum of Natural History, 1988

Mammals

Burt, W., *Mammals of the Great Lakes Region*. Ann Arbor: University of Michigan, 1972

Gottschang, J., *A Guide to the Mammals of Ohio*. Columbus: Ohio State University Press, 1981.

Amphibians and Reptiles

Tyning, T.F., *A Guide to Amphibians and Reptiles*. Boston: Little, Brown and Co., 1990

Pfingsten, R. and F. Downs, editors, *Salamanders of Ohio*, Columbus, Ohio State University. Ohio Biological Survey, 1989

Ohio's Amphibians. Columbus: Ohio Department of Natural Resources, 1990

Ohio's Reptiles. Columbus: Ohio Department of Natural Resources, 1990

Fishes

Trautman, M., *The Fishes of Ohio*. Columbus: Ohio State University Press, 1981

Insects

Iftner, D., J. Shuey, and J. Calhoun, editors, *Butterflies and Skippers of Ohio*. Columbus: Ohio State University. Ohio Biological Survey, 1992.

Graves, R. and D. Brzoska, editors, *The Tiger Beetles of Ohio*. Columbus: Ohio State University. Ohio Biological Survey, 1991

Archeology

Prufer, O. and D. McKenzie, editors, *Studies in Ohio Archeology*. Kent: Kent State University Press, 1975.

General Natural History

Palmer, E., *Fieldbook of Natural History*. New York: McGraw-Hill Book Co., 1975

Lafferty, M., editor, *Ohio's Natural Heritage*. Columbus: The Ohio Academy of Science, 1979.

Lake County Bird List

The following list of Lake County birds is meant to be a guide to the birds which breed in select Lake County habitats. The list is not comprehensive nor are all the species listed restricted to the habitat they are listed under. Backyard birds are those species which might be encountered at a bird feeder or breeding in the suburban yard. Birds marked by an asterisk are permanent residents.

The birds listed in the migrants section are species which can be encountered throughout the county in passage but do not breed here. Some species will have ranges restricted to suitable foraging habitat, for example, diving ducks on Lake Erie. Other species can be encountered almost anywhere in the county, i.e. waves of wood warblers passing through in May.

Birds of the Mature Forests

Cooper's Hawk*

Red-shouldered Hawk*

Broad-winged Hawk

Ruffed Grouse*

Eastern Screech Owl*

Great-horned Owl*

Barred Owl *

Red-headed Woodpecker

Red-bellied Woodpecker*

Hairy Woodpecker*

Downy Woodpecker*

Northern Flicker

Pileated Woodpecker*

Eastern Wood-Pewee

Acadian Flycatcher

Eastern Phoebe

Great-crested Flycatcher

Blue Jay*

American Crow*

Black-capped Chickadee*

Tufted Titmouse*

White-breasted Nuthatch*

Wood Thrush

Veery

Eastern Robin

Solitary Vireo

Yellow-throated Vireo

Red-eyed Vireo

Black-throated Green Warbler

Cerulean Warbler

American Redstart

Ovenbird

Louisiana Waterthrush

Hooded Warbler

Scarlet Tanager

Northern Cardinal*

Rose-breasted Grosbeak

Open Field Habitats

Turkey Vulture

Red-tailed Hawk*

American Kestrel*

Ring-necked Pheasant*

Killdeer
Purple Martin
Barn Swallow
Horned Lark
Field Sparrow
Vesper Sparrow
Savannah Sparrow
Grasshopper Sparrow
Bobolink
Red-winged Blackbird
Eastern Meadowlark

Old Field, Shrub, Woodland Edge & Successional Habitats

Ruffed Grouse*
American Woodcock
Rock Dove*
Mourning Dove*
Black-billed Cuckoo
Yellow-billed Cuckoo
Eastern Screech-Owl*
Great Horned Owl*
Ruby-throated Hummingbird
Northern Flicker
Willow Flycatcher
Eastern Kingbird
American Crow*
House Wren
Blue-gray Gnatcatcher
Eastern Bluebird
Gray Catbird
Brown Thrasher
Warbling Vireo

Old Field, Shrub, etc. continued

Blue-winged Warbler
Yellow Warbler
Common Yellowthroat
Indigo Bunting
Rufous-sided Towhee
Field Sparrow
Song Sparrow*
Common Grackle
Brown-Headed Cowbird
Northern Oriole
American Goldfinch*

Aquatic Habitats

Great Blue Heron
Green-backed Heron
Black-crowned Night Heron
American Bittern
Least Bittern
Canada Goose*
Wood Duck
American Black Duck
Mallard
Virginia Rail
Sora
Common Moorhen
Spotted Sandpiper
Belted Kingfisher
Alder Flycatcher
Eastern Phoebe
Northern Rough-winged Swallow
Bank Swallow
Tree Swallow

Marsh Wren
Warbling Vireo
Northern Yellowthroat
Swamp Sparrow
Red-winged Blackbird

Backyard Birds

Rock Dove *
Mourning Dove*
Eastern Screech Owl*
Chimney Swift
Ruby-throated Hummingbird
Red-bellied Woodpecker*
Hairy Woodpecker*
Downy Woodpecker *
Northern Flicker
Eastern Phoebe
Barn Swallow
Blue Jay *
American Crow*
Black-capped Chickadee*
Tufted Titmouse*
White-breasted Nuthatch*
Carolina Wren *
House Wren
American Robin
Cedar Waxwing
European Starling*
Northern Cardinal *
Chipping Sparrow
Song Sparrow*
Common Grackle

Backyard Birds continued
Brown-headed Cowbird
Northern Oriole
Purple Finch
House Finch *
American Goldfinch*
House Sparrow*

Migrants

Common Loon
Pied-billed Grebe
Horned Grebe
Double-crested Cormorant
Great Egret
Black-crowned Night Heron
Tundra Swan
Green-winged Teal
Northern Pintail
Blue-winged Teal
Northern Shoveler
Gadwall
American Wigeon
Canvasback
Redhead
Ring-necked Duck
Greater Scaup
Lesser Scaup
Surf Scoter
Black Scoter
White-winged Scoter
Common Goldeneye
Bufflehead

Hooded Merganser
Common Merganser
Red-breasted Merganser
Ruddy Duck
Osprey
Bald Eagle
Northern Harrier
Sharp-shinned Hawk
Rough-legged Hawk
Merlin
Peregrine Falcon
American Coot
Black-bellied Plover
Lesser Golden Plover
Semipalmated Plover
Greater Yellowlegs
Lesser Yellowlegs
Solitary Sandpiper
Willet
Whimbrel
Ruddy Turnstone
Sanderling
Semipalmated Sandpiper
Western Sandpiper
Least Sandpiper
White-rumped Sandpiper
Baird's Sandpiper
Pectoral Sandpipe
Purple Sandpiper
Dunlin
Stilt Sandpiper
Short-billed Dowitcher

Long-billed Dowitcher
Common Snipe
Bonaparte's Gull
Ring-billed Gull
Herring Gull
Great Black-backed Gull
Caspian Tern
Common Tern
Forster's Tern
Black Tern
Yellow-bellied Sapsucker
Yellow-bellied Flycatcher
Least Flycatcher
Red-breasted Nuthatch
Brown Creeper
Winter Wren
Golden-crowned Kinglet
Ruby-crowned Kinglet
Gray-cheeked Thrush
Swainson's Thrush
Hermit Thrush
Northern Shrike
White-eyed Vireo
Philadelphia Vireo
Tennessee Warbler
Nashville Warbler
Northern Parula
Chestnut-sided Warbler
Magnolia Warbler
Cape May Warbler
Black-throated Blue Warbler
Yellow-rumped Warbler

Blackburnian Warbler

Pine Warbler

Palm Warbler

Bay-Breasted Warbler

Blackpoll Warbler

Black-and-white Warbler

Northern Waterthrush

Mourning Warbler

Wilson's Warbler

Canada Warbler

Fox Sparrow

American Tree Sparrow

Lincoln's Sparrow

White-throated Sparrow

White-crowned Sparrow

Dark-eyed Junco

Lapland Longspur

Snow Bunting

Common Redpoll

Pine Siskin

Rusty Blackbird

Evening Grosbeak

Mammals of Lake County

Pouched Mammals
Virginia opossum

Insectivores
masked shrew

smoky shrew

short-tailed shrew

least shrew

hairy-tailed mole

star-nosed mole

Bats
little brown myotis

silver-haired bat

eastern pipistrelle

big brown bat

Keen's myotis

Indiana myotis

red bat

hoary bat

Rabbits and Hares
eastern cottontail

Hoofed Mammals
white-tailed deer

Rodents
eastern chipmunk

groundhog (woodchuck)

gray squirrel

fox squirrel

red squirrel

southern flying squirrel

beaver

deer mouse

white-footed mouse

meadow vole

woodland vole

muskrat

southern bog lemming

Norway rat

house mouse

meadow jumping mouse

woodland jumping mouse

Carnivores
coyote

red fox

gray fox

raccoon

short-tailed weasel

long-tailed weasel

least weasel

mink

striped skunk

Amphibians and Reptiles of Lake County

Amphibians

Salamanders
mudpuppy

Jefferson salamander

spotted salamander

marbled salamander

silvery salamander

small-mouthed salamander

Jefferson hybrid salamander

red-spotted newt

northern duskey salamander

Allegheny mountain salamander

four-toed salamander

two-lined salamander

red-backed salamander

slimy salamander

northern red salamander

Toads and Frogs
American toad

Fowler's toad

gray tree frog

northern spring peeper

bull frog

green frog

pickerel frog

northern leopard frog

wood frog

Reptiles

Turtles
snapping turtle

midland painted turtle

spotted turtle

Blanding's turtle

map turtle

eastern spiny soft shell turtle

Lizard
five-lined skink

Snakes
blue racer

black racer

intergrade racer

northern ringneck snake

black rat snake

eastern milk snake

northern water snake

northern brown snake

northern red-bellied snake

eastern ribbon snake

eastern garter snake

Fishes of Lake County

* Lake Erie   O Ponds/Streams   @ Both

@ silver lamprey
O northern brook lamprey
@ sea lamprey
@ American brook lamprey
* lake sturgeon
@ longnose gar
@ bowfin
* alewife
@ gizzard shad
@ Chinook salmon
@ Coho salmon
O brook trout
O brown trout
@ rainbow trout
* lake trout
* Lake Erie cisco
* lake whitefish
* rainbow smelt
O central mudminnow
O chain pickerel
O grass pickerel
@ northern pike
@ great lake muskellunge
@ common carp
@ gold fish
@ golden shiner
O river chub
@ silver chub
O northern bigeye chub
O western blacknose dace
@ longnose dace
O northern creek chub
O southern redbelly dace
O redside dace
O pugnose minnow

@ emerald shiner
O silver shiner
O rosyface shiner
O northern redfin shiner
O central striped shiner
O common shiner
* spottail shiner
O spotfin shiner
@ sand shiner
@ northern mimic shiner
O silverjaw minnow
O northern flathead minnow
@ bluntnose minnow
@ central stoneroller minnow
@ quillback carpsucker
O silver redhorse
@ black redhorse
@ golden redhorse
@ northern shorthead redhorse
@ river redhorse
O northern hog sucker
@ common white sucker
O spotted sucker
O western lake chubsucker
@ channel catfish
O yellow bullhead
@ brown bullhead
@ black bullhead
@ stonecat madtom
O brindled madtom
@ trout perch
* burbot
O brook silverside
O brook stickleback
@ white bass

* white perch
@ white crappie
@ black crappie
@ northern rockbass
@ northern smallmouth black bass
O northern largemouth black bass
O warmouth sunfish
O green sunfish
@ northern bluegill sunfish
@ pumpkinseed sunfish
O orange spotted sunfish
O northern longear sunfish
* sauger
@ walleye

* bluepike (considered extinct)
@ yellow perch
O blackside darter
* channel darter
O Ohio log perch
@ northern logperch
O eastern sand darter
O central johnny darter
* scaly johnny darter
O rainbow darter
O barred fantail darter
@ fresh water drum
O central mottled sculpin
* northern mottled sculpin
O greenside darter
O mooneye

Space does not permit the listing of all categories of plants found in Lake County. Currently, over 2,000 vascular plants have been documented. A comprehensive checklist of Lake County flora to date is on record in the botany department of The Cleveland Museum of Natural History. The following lists are a guide to the common and easily identified trees and wildflowers found in Lake County.

Native Trees of Lake County

eastern hemlock	white oak
white pine	chestnut oak
red cedar	bur oak
black willow	swamp white oak
heartleaf willow	red oak
peach-leaf willow	black oak
shining willow	scarlet oak
swamp cottonwood	pin oak
eastern cottonwood	shingle oak
bigtooth aspen	slippery elm
quaking aspen	American elm
butternut	red mulberry
black walnut	cucumber magnolia
bitternut	tulip-tree (tulip-poplar)
shagbark hickory	pawpaw
big shellbark hickory	sassafras
mockernut hickory	witch-hazel
sweet pignut hickory	sycamore
pignut hickory	wild crab
hop-hornbeam	hawthorn
hornbeam	wild plum
yellow birch	pin cherry
gray birch	wild black cherry
sweet birch	choke cherry
American beech	honey locust
American chestnut	wafer ash

Native Trees continued

smooth sumac

staghorn sumac

poison sumac

red maple

silver maple

sugar maple
(including black maple)

mountain maple

box-elder

Ohio buckeye

American basswood

black gum

pagoda tree
(alternate-leaved dogwood)

flowering dogwood

white ash

green ash

black ash

pumpkin ash

Allegheny serviceberry

downy serviceberry

speckled alder

nannyberry viburnum

Common Naturalized Trees of Lake County

black alder

apple

European mountain ash

European birch

umbrella catalpa

mahaleb cherry

sweet cherry

horse chestnut

Chinese elm

black locust

Norway maple

white mulberry

osage orange

peach

pear

red pine

Scotch pine

oriental plane tree

balm-of-gilead

poplar

Lombardy poplar

white poplar

redbud

rhododendron
(locally naturalized on
conglomerate ledges)

spindle tree

Norway spruce

tree of heaven

English walnut

basket willow

crack willow

weeping willow

white willow

Lake County Ferns and Fern Allies

Ferns

cinnamon fern

royal fern

interrupted fern

long beech fern

broad beech fern

Christmas fern

New York fern

Goldie's fern

rock fragile fern

fragile fern

bracken fern

marsh fern

silvery glade fern

narrow-leaved spleenwort

maidenhair fern

maidenhair spleenwort

ebony spleenwort

rattlesnake fern

cut-leaved grape fern

marginal fern

spinulose wood fern

evergreen wood fern

daisy leaf grape fern

adder's tongue fern

rock cap polypody

lance-leaved grape fern

Appalachian gametophyte

sensitive fern

Horse Tails

field horsetail

water horsetail

woodland horsetail

common scouring rush

smooth scouring rush

Clubmosses and Spike mosses

flat-branch tree clubmoss

meadow spikemoss

shining clubmoss

ground pine

staghorn clubmoss

tree club moss

ground cedar

Representative Lake County Wetland and Woodland Wildflowers

Spring Blooming Sequence

Plant/Wildflower	Approximate Blooming Time
skunk cabbage	By March 1 or earlier
harbinger of spring	March 15 - 30
coltsfoot	March 15 - April 1
hepatica	Aprll 1 - 15
trailing arbutus	April 1 - 15
plantain-leaf woodsedge	April 1 - 30
yellow adder's tongue	April 1 - 30
spring beauty	April 1 - 30
wild leek (foliage)	April 1 - 30
sessile bellwort	April 1 - 30
common blue violet	April 1 - 30
round-leaved yellow violet	April 1 - 30
cut-leaved dentaria	April 15 - 30
two-leaved dentaria	April 15 - 30
dwarf ginseng	April 15 - 30
marsh marigold	April 15 - 30
golden ragwort	May 1 - 15
marsh buttercup	May 1 - 15
yellow and white adder's tongue	May 1 - 15
great white trillium	May 1 - 15
red trilllum	May 1 - 15
Dutchman's breeches	May 1 - 15
squirrel corn	May 1 - 15
blue cohosh	May 1 - 15
rue and wood anemones	May 1 - 15
true Solomon's seal	May 1 - 15

Wetland and Woodland Wild Flowers continued

Plant/Wildflower	Approximate Blooming Time
false spikenard	May 1 - 15
large bellwort	May 1 - 15
yellow and blue violets	May 1 - 15
purple spring cress	May 1 - 15
virginia bluebell	May 15 - 30
Jack-in-the-pulpit	May 15 - 30
wild ginger	May 15 - 30
white spring cress	May 15 - 30
foam flower	May 15 - 30
wild blue phlox	May 15 - 30
may apple	May 15 - 30
sweet cicely	May 15 - 30
white baneberry	May 15 - 30
pale violet	May 15 - 30
false Solomon's seal	May 15 - 30
Jacob's ladder	May 15 - 30
golden alexander	May 15 - 30
Canada mayflower	May 15 - 30
Canada violet	May 15 - 30
wild hyacinth	May 15 - 30
trailing euonymus	May 15 - 30
water leaf	May 15 - 30
cow parsnip	Early June

Wetland and Woodland Wild Flowers continued

Plant/Wildflower	Approximate Blooming Time
false spikenard	May 1 - 15
large bellwort	May 1 - 15
yellow and blue violets	May 1 - 15
purple spring cress	May 1 - 15
virginia bluebell	May 15 - 30
Jack-in-the-pulpit	May 15 - 30
wild ginger	May 15 - 30
white spring cress	May 15 - 30
foam flower	May 15 - 30
wild blue phlox	May 15 - 30
may apple	May 15 - 30
sweet cicely	May 15 - 30
white baneberry	May 15 - 30
pale violet	May 15 - 30
false Solomon's seal	May 15 - 30
Jacob's ladder	May 15 - 30
golden alexander	May 15 - 30
Canada mayflower	May 15 - 30
Canada violet	May 15 - 30
wild hyacinth	May 15 - 30
trailing euonymus	May 15 - 30
water leaf	May 15 - 30
cow parsnip	Early June

Native and Naturalized Old Field Plants
Seasonal Progression

Spring (April/May)
ox-eye daisy

tall buttercup

red clover

white clover

alsike clover

blue-eyed grasses (members of the iris family)

Queen Anne's lace (appears only when field is newly disturbed)

Mid-Summer (late June/July/August)
black-eyed Susan

common beard tongue

birdsfoot trefoil

milkweed (occasionally)

Canada thistle

Fall
tall goldenrod

New England aster

panicled aster

ironweed

November 1993

Acknowledgments

This publication was produced in collaboration by The Cleveland Museum of Natural History, Lake Metroparks and The Holden Arboretum. Project managers: Rosemary Szubski and Stephen Madewell.

The framework and mission of the publication were determined by the editor and the editorial committee who represented the sponsoring agencies. Serving on the editorial committee were: J. Mary Taylor, Ph.D., Director, The Cleveland Museum of Natural History; C.W. Eliot Paine, Director, The Holden Arboretum; and Stephen Madewell, Assistant Director, Planning and Natural Resource Management, Lake Metroparks.

When this project was launched, the editorial committee felt that it was important to involve experts who were currently in the field gathering information in Lake County. Several natural history authorities were approached, and they gave generously of their time and expertise in support of this project. They were eager to encourage an understanding of Lake County's natural history and the importance of conservation of natural resources.

Grateful appreciation is extended to the following staff members of The Cleveland Museum of Natural History who contributed text material for this book: Joseph Hannibal, Ph.D., Curator of Invertebrate Paleontology: bedrock and glacial geology texts; James K. Bissell, Curator of Botany and Coordinator of Natural Areas Division: vegetation text and lists; Harvey Webster, Manager of Wildlife Resources Division: wildlife texts including birds, mammals, reptiles, amphibians, and bird lists; Sonja Teraguchi, Ph.D., Curator of Invertebrate Zoology: insect texts; David Brose, Ph.D., former Curator of Archaeology: Native American pre-history text; Timothy Matson, Ph.D., Curator of Vertebrate Zoology: fish, amphibian and reptile lists.

Gretta Pallister, lifelong Lake County resident, naturalist, and dedicated conservationist, provided research and text for the section that includes first settlers, early naturalists and conservationists. Her contributions to the conservation of Lake County's natural assets extend far beyond this publication. A sincere thank you to her for all her efforts to maintain the natural beauty of Lake County.

In addition to the review provided by the editorial committee and by the various contributing writers, many other people read parts of this publication and offered valuable insights, advise and criticism: Paul Spector, Andrew White, Ph.D., Paul Belanger, Ph.D., Martin Rosenberg, Ph.D., Robert Bartolotta, Kevin Palombo, William Hudson, Brian Parsons, Constance Kehs, Mary Jo Madewell, and Linda Hensley. Thank you.

Photographic files and technical support were provided to the editor by the always patient staff in the departments of Publications and Photo/Audio-Visuals at The Cleveland Museum of Natural History. Supplemental graphic and file photographs were also supplied by the contributing authors and their respective departments at the museum. A sincere thank you for all your efforts on behalf of this project.

Members of the Lake Metroparks administrative staff graciously prepared lists, materials and graphic support for this publication: Ed Quinn, John Pogacnik, Chuck Kenzig and Luna Yu - Lin.

Whenever file photos were not available, original photographs of selected Lake County sites were prepared by Jim Smallwood and Stephen Madewell. Some of the shots were truly "cliff hangers." Thank you for filling in the gaps, frequently on very short notice. Timely preparation of proof sheets was generously provided by Riggin Studio.

In addition to shooting photgraphs, Stephen Madewell's efforts in service of this project are immeasurable. His dedication and commitment of time kept this publication on track and moving forward. His tireless assistance and good humor throughout all the planning phases are most gratefully acknowledged and appreciated.

A final thank you to all the unnamed staff, colleagues and friends who offered suggestions, support and encouragement while this publication was in process.

Photographic and Graphic Credits

A special note of acknowledgment is extended to Vance J. Wissinger, Jr. of Westendorf Printing who brought great skill, patience, and painstaking attention to the preparation of all the graphics. Uncredited photographs, charts, and maps in this publication are from the files of The Cleveland Museum of Natural History, Lake Metroparks, or were designed expressly for this project. All others are used with permission.

Key

OBS - Ohio Biological Survey

ODNR - Ohio Department of Natural Resources

ONH - *Ohio's Natural Heritage* (Ohio Academy of Science, publisher, 1979)

HSF - H. Seymour Fowler (*Field Book of Natural History*)

Page 7: ODNR; Pages 11, 12: Vance Wissinger; Pages 13, 14: TV8 Calmanac; Page 19: Joseph Hannibal, Luna Yu-Lin, Vance Wissinger; Page 26: Thomas J. Mitchell; Pages 27, 28: ODNR modified; Page 29: ODNR; Page 30: OBS; Page 38: OBS; Pages 40: ONH; 41: ODNR; Page 42: HSF (hemlock); Page 44: HSF (bracken fern); Page 48: Vance Wissinger (forest layers); Page 49: HSF; Page 50: ONH; Page 51: HSF (Eastern phoebe, Tufted titmouse); Page 52: HSF (bat); Page 53: ODNR (squirrel), USDA Forest Service (shrew); Page 54: ODNR; Page 55: ODNR (red fox); Pages 58, 59 ODNR; Page 60: Bill Hudson (coyote); Page 61: ODNR (ruffed grouse); Page 62: HSF (cecropia moth); Page 64: ODNR (eagle); Page 65: ODNR (herring gull), ODNR (wood duck); Page 66: ODNR (Canada goose); Page 67: ODNR (water strider); Page 68: ODNR (beaver); Page 70: ODNR (fish); Page 71: ODNR; Page 72: Vance Wissinger (chart); Page 73: Lake Erie Indian Museum; Page 74: Gwen King.